Ghost Hunter's Guide
to
Los Angeles

Ghost Hunter's Guide
to
Los Angeles

By Jeff Dwyer

PELICAN PUBLISHING COMPANY
GRETNA 2007

The word "Pelican" and the depiction of a pelican are trademarks
of Pelican Publishing Company, Inc., and are registered in the
U.S. Patent and Trademark Office.

Library of Congress Cataloging-in-Publication Data

Dwyer, Jeff.
  Ghost hunter's guide to Los Angeles / by Jeff Dwyer.
    p. cm.
  Includes index.
  ISBN 978-1-58980-404-3 (pbk. : alk. paper)
  1. Ghosts—California—Los Angeles Region. 2. Haunted places—
California—Los Angeles Region. I. Title.
  BF1472.U6D867 2007
  133.109794'94—dc22
                                                    2006103492

Printed in the United States of America

Published by Pelican Publishing Company, Inc.
1000 Burmaster Street, Gretna, Louisiana 70053

To my wife and partner in many ghost hunts,
Darlene Dwyer,
always ready for an adventure.

Contents

Introduction
to Ghost Hunting

Who believes in ghosts? People from every religion, culture, and generation believe that ghosts exist. The popularity of ghosts and haunted places in books, television programs, and movies reflects a belief held by many that other dimensions and spiritual entities exist.

In 2000, a Gallup poll discovered a significant increase in the number of Americans who believe in ghosts since the question was first asked in 1978. Thirty-one percent of respondents said they believe ghosts exist. In 1978, only 11 percent admitted to believing in ghosts. Less than a year later, Gallup found that 42 percent of the public believed a house could be haunted but only 28 percent believed that we can hear from or mentally communicate with someone who has died. In 2005, a CBS News poll reported similar findings. Twenty-two percent of the respondents admitted they had personally seen or felt the presence of a ghost. Seventy-eight percent said they believe in an afterlife. A 2003 Harris poll found an astounding 51 percent of Americans believe in ghosts. As with preceding polls, belief in ghosts was greatest among females. More young people accepted the idea of ghosts than older people. Forty-four percent of people aged 18-29 years admitted a belief in ghosts compared with 13 percent of those over 65.

In October 2001, Home and Garden TV conducted a survey at its Web site. When asked "Do you believe in ghosts?" 87 percent of respondents said, "Yes!" Fifty-one percent indicated they had seen a ghost but only 38 percent would enter a haunted house alone at night.

Another channel, SciFi, recognized the phenomenal interest in paranormal phenomena and launched a weekly one-hour primetime program on ghost hunting. SciFi also airs programs that investigate psychic abilities, reincarnation, telekinesis, and many other fascinating topics.

Even the major networks have begun to schedule programming that reflects their audience's interest in the supernatural. NBC broadcasts a weekly primetime drama that follows the experiences of a medium who communicates with ghosts in order to solve crimes, while CBS launched a dramatic series about a woman who acts as the intermediary between spirits and the individuals they haunt.

More than 2,200,000 references to ghosts, ghost hunting, haunted places, or related paranormal phenomena have been discovered through the Internet. Clearly, interest in these areas is widespread.

There is no way of knowing how many people have seen or heard a ghost only to feel too embarrassed, foolish, or frightened to admit it. Many ghost hunters and spiritual investigators believe a vast majority of people have seen or heard something from the other world but failed to recognize it.

The recent worldwide interest in ghosts is not a spin-off of the New Age movement or the current popularity of angels or the manifestation of some new religious process. The suspicion or recognition that ghosts exist is simply the reemergence of one of mankind's oldest and most basic beliefs: there is a life after death.

Ancient writings from many cultures describe apparitions and a variety of spirit manifestations that include tolling bells, chimes, disembodied crying or moaning, and whispered messages. Legends and ancient books include descriptions of ghosts, dwelling places of spirits, and periods of intense spiritual activity related to seasons or community events such as festivals or crop harvests.

Vital interactions between the living and deceased have been described. Many ancient cultures included dead people, or their spirits, in community life. Spirits of the dead were sought as a source of guidance, wisdom, and protection for the living.

Many believers of the world's oldest religions agree that nonliving entities may be contacted for guidance or may be seen on the earthly plane. Among these are visions of saints, the Virgin Mary, and angels.

Ancient sites of intense spiritual activity in Arizona, New Mexico, and Central and South America are popular destinations for travelers seeking psychic or spiritual experiences. More modern, local sites where a variety of paranormal events have occurred are also popular destinations for adventurous living souls. Amateur and professional ghost hunters seek the spirits of the dearly departed in Los Angeles's historic sites, Victorian mansions, old studios, and countless other places around the southland, including graveyards and the attic of your own home. Modern buildings, parks, theatres, and ships, such as the *Queen Mary* in Long Beach, also serve as targets for ghost hunters.

Throughout the past two millennia, the popularity of belief in ghosts has waxed and waned, similar to religious activity. When a rediscovery of ghosts and their role in our lives occurs, skeptics label the notion a fad or an aberration of modern lifestyles. Perhaps people are uncomfortable with the idea that ghosts exist because it involves an examination of our nature and our concepts of life, death, and afterlife. These concepts are most often considered in the context of religion, yet ghost hunters recognize that acceptance of the reality of ghosts, and a life after death, is a personal decision, having nothing to do with religious beliefs or church doctrine. An intellectual approach enables the ghost hunter to explore haunted places without religious bias or fears.

The greater frequency of ghost manifestations in the Los Angeles area, as evidenced by documentary reports on TV and other news media, reflects some people's open-mindedness and widespread interest in ghostly experiences. Ghost hunting is becoming a weekend pastime for many adventurous souls. Advertisement of haunted inns, restaurants, and historical sites is commonplace. It is always fun, often very exciting, and may take ghost hunters places they never dreamed of going.

ABOUT THIS BOOK

Chapter 1 of this book will help you, the ghost hunter, research and organize your own ghost hunt. Chapters 2 through 6 describe several locations at which ghostly activity has been reported. Unlike other collections of ghost stories and descriptions of haunted places, this book emphasizes access. Addresses of each haunted site are included along with other information to assist you in locating and entering the location. Several appendixes offer organizational material for your ghost hunts, including a Sighting Report Form to document your adventures, lists of suggested reading and videos, and organizations you may contact about your experiences with ghosts.

GHOST HUNTING IN THE LOS ANGELES AREA

The very word *ghost* immediately brings to mind visions of ancient European castles, foggy moors, and dark, wind-swept ramparts where brave knights battled enemies of the crown or heroines threw themselves to their death rather than marry the evil duke. The fact is that ghosts are everywhere. A history based in antiquity that includes dark dungeons, hidden catacombs and graveyards, or ancient ruins covered with a veil of sorrow and pain is not essential.

Indeed, Los Angeles and the surrounding communities have all the ingredients necessary for successful ghost hunting. The region has been populated for 200 years with people from a variety of cultures who experienced tremendous changes in their lives. These include the arrival of Spanish colonists in 1771, military campaigns of the Mexican period (1820-46), the gold rush of 1849, the oil boom of the 1890s, and earthquakes, fires, and other disasters of the 20th century.

Throughout the southland's history there have been countless opportunities for the spirits of the dearly departed to feel a need to stay on. There are many old hotels and restaurants, neighborhoods, forts, barrooms, Spanish missions, movie studios, and ships inhabited by ghosts who can be seen or sensed. These lost souls are often the result of violent or unexpected death, often at an early age. These unfortunate people passed with great emotional anguish, leaving their souls with a desire for a completion of their life's objectives or a sense of obligation to offer protection to a particular place. Some ghosts remain on the earthly plane to provide guidance for someone still alive, or for revenge.

Los Angeles has had its share of criminal activities and social injustice.

This has produced many disadvantaged, used, abused, and forlorn people who remain with us after their death. Their souls seek lost dreams while they remain attached to what little they gained during their difficult lives. Many ghosts, harboring resentment, pain, a sense of loss, or a desire to complete their unfinished business, still roam the darkened halls of Victorian mansions, hotels, theatres, neglected cemeteries, modern buildings, and many other places throughout the region that are accessible to the public.

WHAT IS A GHOST?

A ghost is some aspect of the personality, spirit, consciousness, energy, mind, or soul that remains after the body dies. When any of these are detected by the living—through sight, sound, odor, or movement—the manifestation is called an apparition by parapsychologists. The rest of us call it a ghost. How the ghost manifests itself is unknown. There seems to be a close association, however, between aspects of the entity's life and its manifestation as a ghost. These include a sudden, traumatic death, strong ties either to loved ones who survived the entity or to a particular place, unfinished business, strong emotions such as hatred and anger, or a desire for revenge.

Ghosts differ from other paranormal phenomena by their display of intelligent action. This includes interaction with the living, performance of a purposeful activity, or a response to ongoing changes in the environment. Ghosts may speak to the living, warning of a foreseen accident or disaster, giving advice, or expressing their love, anger, remorse, or disappointment. They may try to complete some project or duty they failed to complete before death. Some ghosts try to move furniture, room decorations, and the like to suit their preferences.

Some ghosts appear solid and function as living beings because they are unaware they are dead. Others appear as partial apparitions because they are confused about the transition from life to death.

Occasionally, paranormal activity is bizarre, frightening, or dangerous to witnesses. Objects may fly about, strange sounds may be heard, or accidents happen. This kind of activity is attributed to a poltergeist, or noisy ghost. Most authorities believe that a living person, not the dead, causes these manifestations. Generally, someone under great emotional stress releases psychic energy that creates subtle or spectacular changes in the environment.

Noises commonly associated with a poltergeist include tapping on walls or ceilings, heavy footsteps, shattered glass, the ringing of telephones, and running water. Objects may move about on tables or floors or fly across a room. Furniture may spin or tip over. Dangerous objects such as knives, hammers, or pens may hit people. These poltergeist events can last from only a few days to a year or more. Discovery and removal of the emotionally unstable, living agent often terminates them.

HAUNTINGS

Hauntings and apparitions may not be the same thing. In fact, some professional ghost hunters and parapsychologists make a clear distinction between these two kinds of paranormal phenomena. They share many of the same features in terms of what witnesses see, feel, or smell, but a haunting may occur without the presence of a spiritual entity or consciousness of a dead person. People have reported seeing the pale, transparent images of the deceased walking in hallways, climbing stairs, or sitting in rocking chairs or seats in airplanes, trains, buses, and restaurants. Some have been seen sleeping in beds, hanging by a rope from a tree, or walking through walls. Most commonly, a partial apparition is seen, but witnesses have reported seeing entire armies engaged in battle. Unlike ghosts, hauntings do not display intelligent action with respect to the location. They don't manipulate your new computer, and they do not interact with the living.

Hauntings may be environmental imprints or recordings of something that happened at a location as a result of the repetition of intense emotion. As such, they tend to be associated with a specific place or object, not a particular person. The ghostly figures tend to perform some kind of task or activity that is repetitive. Sometimes the haunting is so repetitive that witnesses feel as though they are watching a video loop that plays the same brief scene over and over. A good example is the image of a deceased grandmother who makes appearances seated in her favorite rocking chair. Another is John Pedder, crewman on the *Queen Mary*. His image is often seen sliding under the watertight door that crushed him during a routine drill.

There is much evidence that people can trigger and experience these environmental recordings by visiting the particular site, touching an object that was a key element of the event, and psychically connecting with the event. Images of hauntings have been picked up on still and video film and digital recordings. The location of strong environmental imprints can also be discovered through devices such as electromagnetic field detectors. Higher magnetic readings have been found at locations where psychics frequently experience hauntings.

HOW DOES A GHOST MANIFEST ITSELF?

Ghosts interact with our environment in a variety of ways that may have something to do with the strength of their personality, level of confusion concerning their transformation by death, talents or skills they possessed in life, personal objectives, or level of frustration in getting our attention. Some ghosts create odors or sounds, particularly those associated with their habits, such as cigar smoke or whistling. The odors of tobacco, oranges, and hemp are most commonly reported. Sounds, including voice messages, may be detected with an audio recorder (see Audio Recording Techniques in chapter 1). Ghost hunters have recorded greetings, warnings, screams, sobbing, and expressions of love.

One of the most common ghostly activities is moving objects. Ghosts like to knock over stacks of cards or coins, turn doorknobs, scatter matchsticks, and move your keys. For many, it appears easy to manipulate light switches and TV remotes, move windows or doors, or push chairs around. Some ghosts have the power to throw objects, pull pictures from a wall, or move heavy items. As a rule, ghosts cannot tolerate disturbances within the place they haunt. If you tilt a wall-mounted picture, the ghost will set it straight. Obstacles placed in the ghost's path may be pushed aside. These seemingly minor indications of ghostly activity should be recorded for future reference on the Sighting Report Form in Appendix A.

Ghosts can also create changes in the physical qualities of an environment. Ice cold breezes and unexplained gusts of wind are often the first signs that a ghost is present. Moving or stationary cold spots, with temperatures several degrees below surrounding areas, have been detected with reliable instruments. Temperature changes sometimes occur along with a feeling sensed by witnesses that the atmosphere has thickened as if the room were suddenly filled with unseen people.

Devices that detect changes in magnetic, electrical, or radio fields have been used in the search for ghosts. However, detected changes may be subject to error, interference by other electrical devices, or misinterpretation. Measurements indicating the presence of a ghost may be difficult to capture on a permanent record.

Ghosts may create images on still cameras (film or digital) and video recorders, such as luminous fogs, balls of light called orbs, streaks of light, or the partial outline of body parts. In the 1860s this was called "spirit photography." Modern digital photographs are easily edited and make it difficult to produce convincing proof of ghostly activity.

Humanoid images are the prized objective of most ghost hunters but they are the least to be experienced. When such images occur, they are often partial, revealing only a head and torso with an arm or two. The feet are seldom seen and full-body apparitions are extremely rare. The solidity of these images is highly variable. Some ghost hunters have seen ethereal, fully transparent forms that are barely discernible while others report ghosts who appear as solid as a living being.

WHY DO GHOSTS REMAIN IN A PARTICULAR PLACE?

Ghosts remain in a particular place because they are emotionally attached to a room, a building, activities, events, or special surroundings that profoundly affected them during their lives, or played a role in their death. A prime example is the haunted house inhabited by the ghost of a man who hung himself in the master bedroom because his wife left him. It is widely believed that death and sudden transition from the physical world confuse a ghost. He or she remains in familiar or emotionally stabilizing surroundings to ease the strain. A place-bound ghost is most likely to exist when a violent death occurred with great emotional anguish. Ghosts may linger in a house, barn, cemetery, factory, or store waiting for a loved one or anyone familiar who might help them deal with their new level of existence. Some ghosts wander through buildings or forests, on bridges, or alongside particular sections of roads. Some await enemies seeking revenge. Others await a friend and a chance for resolution of their guilt.

UNDER WHAT CONDITIONS IS A SIGHTING MOST LIKELY?

Although ghosts may appear at any time, a sighting may occur on special holidays, anniversaries, birthdays, or during historic periods (July 4, December 7) or calendar periods pertaining to the personal history of the ghost. Halloween is reputed to be a favorite night for many apparitions, while others seem to prefer their own special day, or night, on a weekly or monthly cycle.

Night is a traditional time for ghost activity, yet experienced ghost hunters know that sightings may occur at any time. There seems to be no consistent affinity of ghosts for darkness, but they seldom appear when artificial light is bright. Perhaps this is why ghosts shy away from camera crews and their array of lights. Ghosts seem to prefer peace and quiet, although some of them have been reported to make incessant, loud sounds. Even a small group of ghost hunters may make too much noise to facilitate a sighting. For this reason, it is recommended that you limit your group to four persons and oral communication be kept to a minimum.

IS GHOST HUNTING DANGEROUS?

No. Ghost hunting is not dangerous. Motion pictures and children's ghost stories have created a widespread notion that ghosts may inflict harm or even cause the death of persons they dislike. There are a few reports of ghosts attacking people but these are highly suspect. Persons who claim to have been injured by a ghost have, in most cases, precipitated the injury themselves through their own ignorance or fear. The ghost of the Abbot of Trondheim was reputed to have attacked some people decades ago, but circumstances and precipitating events are unclear. Authorities believe that rare attacks by ghosts are a matter of mistaken identity, i.e., the ghost misidentified a living person as a figure known to the ghost during his life.

It is possible that attacks may be nothing more than clumsy efforts by a ghost to achieve recognition. Witnesses of ghost appearances have found themselves in the middle of gunfights, major military battles, and other violent events yet sustained not the slightest injury. If the ghost hunter keeps a wary eye and a calm attitude and sets aside tendencies to fear the ghost or the circumstances of its appearance, he will be safe.

Most authorities agree that ghosts do not travel. Ghosts will not follow you home, take up residence in your car, or attempt to occupy your body. They are held in a time and space by deep emotional ties to an event or place. Ghosts have been observed on airplanes, trains, buses, and ships, however. It is unlikely that the destination interests them. Something about the journey, some event such as a plane crash or train wreck, accounts for their appearance as travelers.

HOT SPOTS FOR GHOSTLY ACTIVITY

Numerous sites of disasters, criminal activity, suicides, huge fires, and other tragic events abound in the greater Los Angeles area, providing hundreds of opportunities for ghost hunting. You may visit the locations described in chapters 2 through 6 to experience ghostly activity discovered by others or discover a hot spot to research and initiate your own ghost hunt.

Astute ghost hunters often search historical maps, drawings, and other documents to find the sites of military conflicts, buildings that no longer exist, or locations of tragic events now occupied by modern structures. For example, maps and drawings on display in the old Spanish missions point to the location of mass graves that may lie under parking lots, streets, or other structures. At historic places such as the Banning Home in southwest L.A. and Drum Barracks in Long Beach, old photographs can help you locate the former sites of wells, barns, shacks for ranch hands, barracks for soldiers, and other places to stage a ghost hunt.

Earthquakes have resulted in a large number of sudden and tragic deaths in Southern California. In 1812, a huge earthquake killed 40 people at Mission San Juan Capistrano and seriously damaged mission buildings at Ventura and San Diego. Another major quake struck in 1870 killing over a hundred people and destroying buildings that had literally been constructed with blood, sweat, and tears, mostly by local Indians.

More recently, the Northridge earthquake of January 17, 1994, killed more than 60 persons, collapsed major freeways, and destroyed hundreds of homes. People who died in the earthquake or in its aftermath may haunt the site of their cherished homes, favorite bar or restaurant, or even workplace.

Many adobe missions exist throughout Southern California with present structures dating from the early 1800s. Most of them are beautifully restored and open to the public. The grounds of these monuments to California's Spanish and Mexican periods comprise mass burial sites for thousands of Indians. Many lost their culture, language, religion, and freedom under the harsh rule of Spain and the mission fathers. Mission San Gabriel Arcangel, Mission San Juan Capistrano, Mission San Buena Ventura, and Mission San Fernando Rey de Espana in San Fernando Valley possess fascinating histories and an ambience conducive to ghost hunting.

The homes of many Southern California pioneers, such as the Phineas Banning house in Wilmington, the Doheny Mansion, and the Avila Adobe in central L.A. are reputed to harbor ghosts. Other historic homes such as the Monroe House in Monrovia, Rancho Los Cerritos Adobe in Long Beach, and the Ware-Stanley House in Garden Grove have curious histories and ghostly atmospheres. Of course, San Diego's world-famous Whaley House and Santa Barbara's Big Yellow House are well known for ghostly activity. Some of these charming old homes have become bed-and-breakfast inns, museums, or restaurants, making them exciting weekend destinations for ghost hunters.

Several historic military sites in Southern California are believed to harbor ghosts. At one time, the Union army headquarters at Drum Barracks in Wilmington occupied 60 acres and included the finest hospital in the West. About 17,000 troops trained here from 1861 to

1865 and many went on to see action against the Confederate army in New Mexico and Texas. Today, Drum Barracks is reduced to a single building that served as quarters for junior officers. The site of the hospital is occupied by modern structures and presents a great opportunity for ghost hunters with a flare for historical research.

Fort MacArthur in San Pedro is also greatly reduced from its original span of several hundred acres. Two huge gun emplacements with connecting passageways, powder rooms, and galleries still echo the sounds of gunnery officers and troops who protected L.A. harbor from 1914 to 1977. Some ghost hunters believe spirit remnants from the Spanish period can be detected here as well.

Several cemeteries dating from the 19th century are scattered about the Los Angeles area, many of them quite small and tucked away in seldom-visited areas with unattended graves and forgotten decedents. Westwood Memorial Park, Woodlawn in Santa Monica, and Sunnyside in Long Beach contain the remains of particularly interesting people, including criminals, movie stars, and pioneers.

Among the most fascinating cemeteries in the southland is Hollywood Forever in West L.A. This place is "home" to 88,000 dead people, including screen stars such as Rudolph Valentino, producers such as Cecil B. DeMille, and comic talents like Mel Blanc. On summer weekends, as many as 1,700 living guests join the dead. Visitors unfurl blankets among the headstones, spread out gourmet picnic dinners, and enjoy old movies projected onto the wall of the mausoleum. An evening among dead film stars makes perfect sense to people fascinated by the movie industry. For those looking for a fun, spooky evening, this cemetery is perfect.

Information about large construction projects may point you in the direction of a haunted site. The huge Playa Vista project north of Marina del Rey in west Los Angeles includes apartments, condominiums, business venues, and open space. Late in 2003, construction was halted when the bones of more than 300 Native Americans were uncovered and removed. Archeological and historical research revealed that this area was once an important center of Native American culture. In addition to burial artifacts, remnants of at least one large village, including jewelry, eating utensils, and arrowheads, have been found. Construction projects that disturb ancient graves often lead to paranormal phenomena in modern structures placed on the site. Spirits of the dead hate to see their remains unearthed and relocated.

TWO SIMPLE RULES

Two simple rules apply for successful ghost hunting. The first is to be patient. Ghosts are everywhere, but contact may require a considerable investment of time. The second rule is to have fun.

You may report your ghost hunting experiences or suggest hot spots for ghost hunting to the author via e-mail at HJDDwyer@msn.com or by visiting the Web site www.ghostreport.com.

Ghost Hunter's Guide
to
Los Angeles

CHAPTER 1

How to Hunt for Ghosts

You may want to visit recognized haunted sites, listed in chapters 2 through 6, using some of the ghost hunting techniques described later in this chapter. Or you may want to conduct your own spirit investigation. If that is the case, choose a place you think might be haunted, like an old house in your neighborhood or a favorite bed-and-breakfast inn. You may get a lead from fascinating stories about ancestors that have been passed down through your family.

Your search for a ghost, or exploration of a haunted place, starts with research. Summaries of obscure and esoteric material about possible haunted sites are available from museums, local historical societies, and bookstores. Brochures and booklets, sold at historical sites under the California State Park system, can be good resources, too.

Guided tours of historical sites such as the old adobe buildings of Olvera Street, the *Queen Mary* in Long Beach, Spanish missions in San Gabriel and Ventura, or famous Hollywood studios are good places to begin your research. Tours can help you develop a feel for places within a building where ghosts might be sighted or an appreciation of relevant history.

In addition, touring haunted buildings offers you an opportunity to speak with guides and docents who may be able to provide you with clues about the dearly departed or tell you ghost stories you can't find in published material. Docents may know people—old-timers in the area or amateur historians—who can give you additional information about a site, its former owners or residents, and its potential for ghostly activity.

Almost every city has a local historical society (see Appendix G).

These are good places to find information that may not be published anywhere else, such as histories of local families and buildings, information about tragedies, disasters, criminal activity, or legends and myths about places that may be haunted. You will want to take notes about secret scandals or other ghost-producing happenings that occurred at locations now occupied by modern buildings, roads, or parks. In these cases, someone occupying a new house or other structure could hear strange sounds, feel cold spots, or see ghosts or spirit remnants.

Newspapers are an excellent source of historical information as well. You can search for articles about ghosts, haunted places, or paranormal activity by accessing the newspaper's archives via the Internet and entering key words, dates, or names. Newspaper articles about suicides, murders, train wrecks, plane crashes, and paranormal phenomena can often provide essential information for your ghost hunt. Stories about authentic haunted sites are common around Halloween.

Bookstores and libraries usually have special-interest sections with books on local history by local writers. A few inquiries may connect you with these local writers who may be able to help you focus your research.

If these living souls cannot help, try the dead. A visit to a local graveyard is always fruitful in identifying possible ghosts. Often you can find headstones that indicate the person entombed died of suicide, criminal activity, local disaster, or such. Some epitaphs may indicate if the deceased was survived by a spouse and children, or died far from home.

Perhaps the best place to start a search for a ghost is within your own family. Oral histories can spark your interest in a particular ancestor, scandal, building, or site relevant to your family. Old photographs, death certificates, letters and wills, anniversary lists in family Bibles, and keepsakes can be great clues. Then you can visit gravesites and/or homes of your ancestors to check out the vibes as you mentally and emotionally empathize with specific aspects of your family's history.

Almost every family has a departed member who died at an early age, suffered hardships and emotional anguish, passed away suddenly due to an accident or natural disaster, or was labeled a skeleton in the family's closet. Once you have focused your research on a deceased person, you need to determine if that person remains on this earthly plane as a ghost.

Evaluate the individual's personal history to see if he had a reason to remain attached to a specific place.

Was his death violent or under tragic circumstances?

Did he die at a young age with unfinished business?

Did the deceased leave behind loved ones who needed his support and protection?

Was this person attached to a specific site or building?

Would the individual be inclined to seek revenge against those responsible for his death?

Would his devotion and sense of loyalty lead him to offer eternal companionship to loved ones?

Revenge, anger, refusal to recognize the reality of transformation by death, and other negative factors prompt many spirits to haunt places and people. However, most ghosts are motivated by positive factors. Spirits may remain at a site to offer protection to a loved one or a particular place.

Also, remember that ghosts can appear as animals or objects. Apparitions of ships, buildings, covered wagons, bridges, and roads by the strictest definitions are phantoms. A phantom is the essence of a structure that no longer exists on the physical plane. Many people have seen houses, cottages, castles, villages, and large ships that were destroyed or sunk years before.

BASIC PREPARATION FOR GHOST HUNTING

If you decide to ghost hunt at night or on a special anniversary make a trip to the site a few days ahead of time. During daylight hours, familiarize yourself with the place and its surroundings. Many historical sites are closed after sunset or crowded at certain times by organized tours.

TWO BASIC METHODS FOR FINDING GHOSTS

Based partly on the kind of paranormal activity reported at a site, the ghost hunter must decide which method or approach will be used. Some will feel competent with a collection of cameras, electromagnetic field detectors, digital thermometers, computers, data recorders, and other high-tech gadgets. These ghost hunters prefer to use the Technical Approach. Others may discover they have an emotional affinity for a particular historic site, a surprising fascination with an event associated with a haunting, or empathy for a deceased person. These ghost hunters may have success with the Psychic Approach. Another consideration is the ghost hunter's goal. Some desire scientific evidence of a ghost while others simply want to experience paranormal activity.

THE TECHNICAL APPROACH

Professional ghost hunters often use an array of detection and recording devices that cover a wide range of the electromagnetic spectrum. This approach is complicated, expensive, and requires technically skilled people to operate the devices. Amateur ghost hunters can get satisfying results with simple audio and video recording devices.

Equipment Preparation

A few days before your ghost hunt, purchase fresh film for your camera and tape for audio recording devices. Test your batteries and bring backup batteries and power packs with you. You should have two types of flashlights: a broad-beam light for moving around a site and a penlight-type flashlight for narrow-field illumination while you make notes or adjust equipment. A candle is a good way to light the site in the least offensive manner to your ghost.

Still-Photography Techniques

Many photographic techniques that work well under normal conditions are inadequate for ghost hunts. That's because ghost hunting is usually conducted under conditions of low ambient light requiring long exposures. Some investigators use a strobe or flash device but they can make the photos look unauthentic.

Practice taking photographs with films of various light sensitivities before you go on your ghost hunt. Standard photographic films of high light sensitivity should be used (ASA of 800 or higher is recommended). At a dark or nearly dark location, mount the camera on a tripod. Try several exposure settings from one to 30 seconds and aperture settings under various low-light conditions.

Make notes about the camera settings that work best under various light conditions. Avoid aiming the camera at a scene where there is a bright light such as a street lamp or an exit sign over a doorway. These light sources may "overflow" throughout your photograph.

Some professional ghost hunters use infrared film. You should consult a professional photo lab technician about this type of film and its associated photographic techniques. Several amateur ghost hunters use Polaroid-type cameras with interesting results. The rapid film developing system of these cameras gives almost instant feedback about your technique and/or success in documenting ghost activities. Ghosts have reportedly written messages on Polaroid film.

Many digital cameras have features that enable automatic exposures at specific intervals, e.g., once every minute. This allows a "hands off" remote photograph record to be made. Repetitive automatic exposures also allow a site to be investigated without the presence of the investigator.

Your equipment should include a stable, lightweight tripod. Hand-held cameras may produce poorly focused photographs when the exposure duration is greater that 1/60 second.

Audio Recording Techniques

Tape recorders provide an inexpensive way to obtain evidence of ghostly activity, particularly electronic voice phenomenon, or EVP. Always test your recorder under conditions you expect to find at the investigation site in order to reduce audio artifact and insure optimal performance of the device.

Does your recorder pick up excessive background noise? This may obscure ghostly sounds. If so, consider upgrading the tape quality and using a microphone equipped with a wind guard.

Use two or more recorders at different locations within the site.

This allows you to verify sounds such as wind against a window and reduce the possibility of ambiguous recordings. You can use sound-activated recorders at a site overnight. They will automatically switch on whenever a sound occurs above a minimum threshold. Be aware that each sound on the tape will start with an annoying artifact, the result of a slow tape speed at the beginning of each recorded segment. The slow tape speed could obscure the sounds made by a ghost.

Remote microphones and monitor earphones allow you to remain some distance from the site and activate the recorder when ghostly sounds are heard. If this equipment is not available, use long-play tape (60-90 minutes), turn the recorder on, and let it run throughout your hunt, whether you remain stationary or walk about the site. This will provide you with a means of making audio notes rather than written notes. A headset with a microphone is especially useful with this technique.

Video Recording

Video recorders offer a wide variety of recording features from time-lapse to auto-start/stop, and autofocus. These features enable you to make surveillance-type recordings over many hours while you are off-site. Consult your user's manual for low-light recording guidelines and always use a tripod and long-duration battery packs.

If you plan to attempt video recording, consider using two recorders, at equal distance from a specific object such as a chair. Arrange the recorders at different angles, preferably 90 degrees from each other.

Another approach you might try is to use a wide-angle setting on camera #1 to get a broad view of a room, porch, or courtyard. On camera #2, use a close-up setting to capture ghostly apparitions at a door, chair, or window.

You may have more success with sequential, manual, or timer-actuated tape runs than a continuous-record technique. If you try this technique, use tape runs of one to five minutes. Practice with the method that interrupts the automatic setting should you need to manually control the recording process. Always use a tripod that can be moved to a new location in a hurry.

High-Tech Equipment

Night vision goggles can be useful in low-light situations. You can see doors and other objects move that you might not otherwise see. These goggles are quite expensive, however.

You can buy devices such as electromagnetic field detectors, infrared thermometers, barometers, and motion detectors at your local electronics store or over the Internet. A good source for high-tech ghost hunting equipment is www.technica.com. Electronic gadgets can be useful and fun, but unless you have a means of recording the output, your reports of anomalies, movement, and apparitions will not be the kind of hard evidence you need to satisfy skeptics.

Other Equipment

Various authorities in the field of ghost hunting suggest the following items to help you mark sites, detect paranormal phenomena, and collect evidence of ghostly activity.

White or colored chalk	Compass
Stopwatch	Steel tape measure
Magnifying glass	First-aid kit
Thermometer	Metal detector
Graph paper for diagrams	Small mirror
Small bell	Plastic bags (for evidence)
Matches	Tape for sealing doors
String	Cross
Bible	Cell phone

THE PSYCHIC APPROACH

The psychic approach relies upon your intuition, inner vision, or emotional connection with a deceased person, object, place, or point of time in history. You don't have to be a trained psychic to use this approach. All of us have some capacity to tap into unseen dimensions.

People who feel the peculiar atmosphere of a distant time, or who believe they can perceive a voice, sound, image, touch, or texture of another dimension, may have psychic abilities that will pay off in a ghost hunt. The Psychic Approach does require an ability to eliminate external and internal distractions and focus your perceptions. If you use this approach, three factors may increase your chances of experiencing ghostly activity.

The first factor is the strength of the emotional imprint or attachment of the deceased for a particular place. The frequency, duration, and consistency of the paranormal phenomena may indicate the strength of the imprint. The strongest imprints are created by intense emotions such as fear, rage, jealously, revenge, or loss, especially if they were repetitive over long periods of time prior to death. Other emotions such as love for a person, a place, or an object may also create a strong imprint. Biographical research may reveal this kind of information, particularly if personal letters or diaries are examined. Old newspaper articles and photographs are useful too.

The second factor is the degree of sensitivity the investigator has for environmental imprints. Knowledge of the key elements and historical context of the entity's death can increase your sensitivity. This includes architectural elements of a home, theatre, airplane or ship, furniture, clothing, weapons, or any implement or artifact of the specific time period. Touching or handling these artifacts, or standing within the historic site, enables ghost hunters to get in touch with the historical moment of the ghost's imprint. A high degree of sensitivity for a past era often generates an odd feeling of being transported through time.

The third factor is sensitivity to or empathy for the ghost's lingering presence at a haunted site. A ghost may be trapped, confused, or have chosen to remain at a site to protect someone or guard something precious. Sensitivity for the ghost's predicament can be increased through knowledge of the entity's personal history such as emotions, motivations, problems, or unfinished business at the time of death. Research of historical sources like newspapers, old photographs, or books can provide this kind of information. Useful, intimate details might be found in letters, suicide notes, diaries, and wills.

Your sensitivity to ghostly environmental imprints and spirit manifestations may be increased by meditation. This is a simple process of relaxing one's physical body to eliminate distracting thoughts and tensions and achieve emotional focus.

Meditation allows you to focus your spiritual awareness and physical mind on a single subject, a place, entity, or historic moment in time. As the subject comes into focus, you can add information obtained from your research. Markers of time or seasons, artifacts or implements, furniture and doorways are a few suggestions. By doing this, you can become aware of unseen dimensions of the world around you that create a feeling as though you have moved through time to a distant era. This process can get you in touch with the place, date, and time pertinent to a ghost's imprint or death. The process also enables you to disregard personal concerns, negative thoughts, and attitudes that may interfere with your concentration on the ghost you seek.

Keep in mind that it is possible to be in a meditative "state" while appearing quite normal.

The process is simple and easy to learn. When you arrive at the site of your ghost hunt, find a place a short distance away to meditate. Three essentials for any effective meditation are comfort, quiet, and concentration.

Comfort: Sit or stand in a relaxed position. Take free and even breaths at a slow rate. Do not alter your breathing pattern so much that you feel short of breath, winded, or lightheaded. Close your eyes if that enhances your comfort or focus on a candle, a tree, or a flower. Do not fall asleep. Proper meditation creates relaxation without decreasing alertness.

Quiet: Meditate in a place away from noises generated by traffic, passersby, radios, slammed doors, and the like. If you are with a group, give each other sufficient personal space. Some people use mantras, repetitive words or phrases, or speak only in their mind in order to facilitate inner calmness.

Mantras are useful to induce a focused state of relaxation but they may disrupt the meditation of a companion if spoken aloud. A

majority of ghost hunters do not believe that mantras are necessary in this instance. They point out that ghost hunting is not like a séance as depicted in old movies. It is not necessary to chant special words, call out to the dead, or invite an appearance "from beyond the grave."
Concentration: First, clear your mind of everyday thoughts, worries, and concerns. This is the most difficult part of the process. Many of us don't want to let go of our stressful thoughts. To help you let go of those thoughts, let the thought turn off its light and fade into darkness. After you clear your mind, some thoughts may reappear. Repeat the process. Slowly turn off the light of each thought until you can rest with a completely cleared mind. This might take some practice. Don't wait until you are on the scene of a ghost hunt before you practice this exercise.

Once your mind is clear, focus on your breathing as you imagine your entire being as a single point of energy driving the breathing process. Then, open yourself. Think only of the entity you seek. Starting with the ghost's identity (if known), slowly expand your focus to include its personal history, the historical era of the ghost's death or creation of the emotional imprint, the reported nature and appearance of the haunting, and any specific ghostly activity.

Acknowledge each thought as you continue relaxed breathing. Find a thought that is most attractive to you, then expand your mind to include your present surroundings. Return slowly to your current place and time. Remain quiet for a minute or two before you resume communication with your companions, then move ahead with the ghost hunt.

GROUP ORGANIZATION AND PREPARATION

It is not necessary to be a believer in spirits or paranormal phenomena in order to see a ghost or experience haunting activities. Indeed, most reports of ghost activities are made by unsuspecting people who never gave the matter much thought. But you should not include people in your group with openly negative attitudes about these things. If you include skeptics, be sure they maintain an open mind and are willing to participate in a positive group attitude.

Keep your group small, limited to four members if possible.

Ghosts have been seen by large groups of people but small groups are more easily managed and likely to be of one mind in terms of objectives and methods.

Meet an hour or more prior to starting the ghost hunt at a location away from the site. Review the history of the ghost you seek and the previous reports of ghost activity at the site. Discuss the group's expectations based on known or suspected ghostly activity or specific research goals. Review possible audio and visual apparitions based on the history of paranormal activity at the site, telekinesis, local temperature changes, and intended methods of identifying or recording these phenomena. Most importantly, agree to a plan of action if a sighting is made by any member of the group.

The first priority for a ghost hunter is to maintain visual or auditory contact without a lot of activity such as making notes. Without breaking contact:

1. Activate recording devices
2. Redirect audio, video, or photographic equipment to focus on the ghost
3. Move yourself to the most advantageous position for listening or viewing the ghostly activity
4. Attract the attention of group members with a code word, hand signal (for example, touch the top of your head), or any action that signals other hunters so they can pick up your focus of attention

Should you attempt to interact with the ghost? Only if the ghost invites you to speak or move. Often, ghost hunter's movement or noise frightens the ghost or interferes with the perception of the apparition.

SEARCHING FOR GHOSTS

There are no strict rules or guidelines for successful ghost hunting except BE PATIENT! Professional ghost hunters sometimes wait several days, weeks, or even months before achieving contact with a ghost. Others have observed full-body apparitions when they least expected it, while concentrating fully on some other activity. Regardless of the depth of your research or preparation, you need to be patient. The serious ghost hunter will anticipate that several trips to a haunted site may be required before some sign of ghostly activity is observed.

If you hunt with a group, you need to establish a communications system in the event that even one member might sight a ghost or experiences some evidence of ghostly activity. Of course, confirmation by a second person is important in establishing validity and credibility. In the previous section, a hand signal (hand to the top of the head) was recommended as a means of informing others that they should direct their eyes and ears to a site indicated by the person in contact with a ghost. Because of this, all ghost hunters need to keep their companions in sight at all times and be aware of hand signals.

An audio signal can often reduce the need for monitoring other ghost hunters for hand signals. Equally important for a group is to establish a method for calling other hunters who may be some distance away. Tugging on a length of string can be an effective signal. So can beeping devices, mechanical "crickets," and flashing penlight signals, i.e., one flash for a cold spot and two flashes for an apparition. Hand-held radios, or walkie-talkies, can also be effective. Some models can send an audio signal or activate flashing lights. Cell phones can be used but the electromagnetic activity may be uninviting to your ghost.

Remaining stationary within a room, gravesite, courtyard, or other confirmed location is often most productive. If a ghost is known to have a favorite chair, bed, or other place within a room, he will appear. Under these conditions, the patient ghost hunter will have a successful hunt.

If your ghost is not known to appear at a specific place within a room or an outdoors area, position yourself to gain the broadest view of the site. A corner of a room is optimal because it allows the ghost unobstructed motion about the place while avoiding the impression of a trap set by uninvited people who occupy his favorite space. If you are outdoors at a gravesite, for instance, position yourself at the base of a tree or in the shadows of a monument to conceal your presence while affording a view of your ghost's grave.

If your ghost is a mobile spirit, moving throughout a house, over a bridge, or about a courtyard or graveyard, you may have no choice but to move around the area. Search for a place where you feel a change in the thickness of the air or a cold spot or detect a peculiar odor.

If you are ghost hunting with others, it may be advantageous to station members of your group at various places in the ghost's haunting grounds and use a reliable system to alert others to spirit activity. Each member could then patrol a portion of the site. Radio or cell phone communications may be essential for this type of ghost hunt.

Once you are on site, the above-described meditation may help you focus and maintain empathy for your ghost. Investigate sounds, even common sounds, as the ghost attempts to communicate with you. Make mental notes of the room temperature, air movement, and the sensations of abrupt change in atmosphere as you move about the site. Changes in these factors may indicate the presence of a ghost.

Pay attention to your own sensations or perceptions, such as the odd feeling that someone is watching you, standing close by, or touching you. Your ghost may be hunting you!

WHAT TO DO WITH A GHOST

On occasion, professional ghost hunters make contact with a ghost by entering a trance and establishing two-way communications. The ghost hunter's companions hear him or her speak but the ghost's voice can only be heard by the trance communicator. Sylvia Browne's book, *Adventures of a Psychic,* describes several of these trance communication sessions. Most ghost encounters are brief with little opportunity to engage the entity in conversation. But the ghost may make gestures or acknowledge your presence through eye contact, a touch on the shoulder, sound, or a movement of an object. The ghost hunter must decide to follow the gestures or direction of a ghost or not.

Many of the 600 ghosts who haunt the *Queen Mary* try to get visitors to follow them to the bowels of the ship, leap over the rail, or waltz across the dance floor. The apparition of the engine room chief barks orders, expecting them to be followed to the letter. In the main ballroom, ghostly parties have been observed. The joyful crowd moves with 1930s music while holding champagne classes high in rousing toasts. As the room fills with laughter, visitors are often invited to join in. The ghost of 18-year-old John Pedder is often seen sliding under watertight door 13. He gestures for visitors to follow just before the door crushes him to death, once again. To date, there are no reports of ill effects by those who have been brave enough to follow these spirits. However, invitations such as this are frightening to most of us.

More often, the ghost's activities are directed at getting the intruder to leave a room, house, or gravesite. If you sense your ghost wants you to leave, most hunters believe it is best not to push one's luck. When you have established the nature of the ghost activity, ascertained that your companions have experienced the activity, taken a few photographs, and run a few minutes of audiotape, it may be time to leave. An experience with an unfriendly ghost can be disturbing.

Residents of haunted houses, and employees of haunted business establishments, often accept the ghost's telekinetic or audio activities without concern. It is part of the charm of a place and may add some fun to working in a spooky building.

AFTER THE GHOST HUNT

Turn off all recorders and remove them to a safe place. Some ghost hunters suspect that ghosts can erase tapes. Label your tapes with the date, time, and location. Use a code number for each tape. Keep a separate record of where the tape was made, date, time, and contents. Place tapes in a waterproof bag with your name, address, telephone number, and a note that guarantees postage in case it is misplaced.

Have photographic film developed at a professional color laboratory. Pros at the lab may help you with cropping and image enhancement. Have copies made of the negatives that contain ghostly images.

All members of the group should meet right after the hunt, away from the site. Each hunter who witnessed ghostly activity or an apparition should make a written or audio statement describing the experience. The form presented in Appendix A is for the group leader to complete. Video and audio recordings made at the site should be reviewed and reconciled with witness statements. Then, plans should be made for a follow-up visit in the near future to the site to confirm the apparition, its nature and form, and the impressions of the initial ghost hunt.

Data about the ghost's location within a site may indicate the optimal conditions for future contact with a ghost. Things to be aware of could be the time of day or night, phase of the moon, season, and degree and size of cold spots as well as form and density of the apparition. Patience and detailed records can help you to achieve the greatest reward for a ghost hunter, unmistakable proof of ghostly activity.

CHAPTER 2

North Los Angeles, Hollywood, and the Valley

LEONIS FAMILY GHOSTS

Leonis Adobe
23537 Calabasas Road
Calabasas 91302
(818) 222-6511

Don Miguel Leonis was once known as the most hated man in California. The Basque rancher earned that title by fighting with his neighbors over property lines, shooting trespassers, and intimidating other ranchers in the area with his crew of Mexican gunfighters.

Don Miguel's holdings included large tracts of land in western San Fernando Valley. His domain was expanded when he married an Indian widow, Espiritu Chijulla. As a wedding gift, Espiritu's family gave Leonis the 1,100-acre Escorpion Rancho that included an adobe house built in 1844, herds of sheep, and several horses.

Soon after his marriage, Don Miguel enlarged and updated the adobe house and watched the birth of his only child, daughter Marcellina. But family life neither reduced his violent outbreaks nor the feuds and squabbles that were a part of his daily life as one of the richest and most hated ranchers in Southern California. Even Marcellina's death from smallpox at age 20 did not cool his blood.

In 1889, Don Miguel made the mistake of driving a heavily laden wagon alone through the Cahuenga Pass. Something or someone spooked the horses, causing the wagon to overturn, crushing Miguel. He was carried to his rancho, where for three days he suffered horribly from his injuries. When Don Miguel Leonis died, in the upstairs bedroom, word spread that his death was no accident: rival ranchers had set a trap to kill Leonis, making it look like an accident.

Today, the Leonis Adobe is a museum restored to the era of the Leonis tragedies. Ghosts of this pioneering family haunt the entire house. In the upstairs bedroom, the ghost of bearded Don Miguel has been seen lying in bed asleep. He appears so lifelike that visitors have reported him to docents, thinking a museum caretaker or visitor slipped into bed for a quick nap. Some visitors have seen him breathe with some difficulty or shake as in a seizure while covered with bloody bandages. Heavy footsteps are often heard in the second-floor hallway, sometimes ending with the slamming of a door or windows. Unusual odors have been detected as well. One ghost hunter described them as rotting flesh.

The apparition of a small woman dressed in black has been seen on the second-floor balcony. This ghost, believed to be Espiritu Chijulla Leonis, creates the sound of light steps in the hallway, on the stairs, and in the kitchen. Often, sobbing is heard as Espiritu vanishes. When her ghost is clearly seen, she is described as cadaverous.

Dark figures, columns of cold air, and creepy feelings have been detected outside the house under the balcony. One worker, during a period of renovation, was spared a serious accident by a pair of strong hands that pulled her away from a balcony railing that would have given way had she leaned on it.

Ghost hunters believe the ghost of Marcellina appears here together with house servants and at least one Mexican gunfighter.

GHOST OF SAM WARNER

Warner Pacific Theatre
6433 Hollywood Boulevard
Hollywood 90048-5310

Jack was the youngest of the four Warner brothers who founded one of Hollywood's great studios, but Sam was the workaholic. It was his energy and vision that spawned the idea of "talking pictures." Others in the industry tried but failed. Some argued that movies

Sam Warner worked tirelessly to build this Hollywood theatre, then dropped dead on the eve of its opening.

should not try to be stage plays with actors speaking lines, guns bang-ing, or horses neighing. But Sam, with brothers Jack, Harry, and Albert, made it happen in 1927.

Talking movies were such a stupendous achievement that the brothers decided they needed a grand theatre in which to present these new talking pictures. So, in addition to producing their first film with sound (*The Jazz Singer,* starring Al Jolson), Sam oversaw the construction of a huge theatre on Hollywood Boulevard. He was involved in every step, including the installation of a speaker system. But construction delays and technical problems became overwhelm-ing as the scheduled premiere of *The Jazz Singer* approached. Sam was so stressed, he walked through the unfinished lobby cursing the building and everything he had tried to accomplish in it. Moments later, he suffered a brain hemorrhage and died on October 5, 1927, at the age of 40.

The next day, Warner Brothers' first talking picture opened in New York and changed the movie industry forever. The grand theatre on Hollywood Boulevard opened April 29, 1929, as a principle out-let for films made at Warner Brothers' studios. At the opening cere-mony, the remaining Warner brothers placed a plaque in the lobby to commemorate Sam's achievements.

Sam was so immersed in the construction of the theatre and the production of talking pictures that he remains on the job at the Warner Pacific Theatre. His ghost is often seen pacing the lobby, fretting about the things that remain to be done. Cleaning staff have seen him walk across the lobby, push the elevator buttons, and enter the elevator. Sam also is seen on the second-floor offices. When he is finished there, he uses the elevator to return to the lobby. If anything is out of place, Sam moves chairs, closes doors, or moves wastebaskets.

Other apparitions have been seen at this historic theatre. A short woman dressed in dark 1920s clothing floats through the long, curv-ing lobby, passing over the spot where Sam Warner collapsed in 1927. On the stairway that descends from the lobby to the lower level, a column of very cold air has been detected. It moves up and down the stairs.

TALENTED GHOSTS OF THE PALACE THEATRE

Vine Street at Hollywood Boulevard
Hollywood 90028
(213) 239-0959

This fascinating old building opened as the Hollywood Playhouse in 1927. Throughout the 1930s and '40s, live radio programs were broadcast from the stage in front of a lively audience. In the 1950s, classic TV programs such as Groucho Marx's *Your Bet Your Life, The Lawrence Welk Show,* and Bob Hope specials were staged here. The place has since been remodeled to include a nightclub and facilities for filming TV specials and showcasing new talent in front of a live audience. Each of the three floors has a lobby, a stage for performers, and a seating area.

The ghosts of the Palace Theatre were first documented in the early 1990s when night security staff heard someone playing the piano on the third floor. The music was beautiful, but at 2:30 A.M. performers were not supposed to be rehearsing. When a guard tried to enter the room, he found the doors locked. As soon as he turned the key, the music stopped. Inside, he found the piano cover had been removed and the bench moved as though someone had just stepped away. There is suspicion that the musician might be a woman.

On the second floor, near the stairs, guards have felt a cold breeze move past them, leaving the scent of perfume. At times, an invisible presence has been felt. One guard felt someone tap him on the shoulder just as cold air surrounded him.

On the first floor, a tall man wearing a tux appears on stage. His feet are not visible and his face appears transparent. Another ghost turns on the stage lights, then floats across the stage. In the balcony overlooking the main dance floor, a man and woman are often seated at a small table. Dressed in 1930s clothing, they carry on an animated conversation as if they are celebrating an important anniversary. They ignore the guards who speak to them and disappear if anyone approaches their table. During special events, patrons on the main floor frequently complain of loud conversations emanating from the empty balcony.

Visitors and staff often hear brief sounds from musical instruments, singers, the applause of invisible audiences, and disembodied voices of performers responding with "Thank you. Thank you very much."

HOLLYWOOD HANGOUT

All Star Theatre Café
1714 North Ivar Avenue
Hollywood 90028
(323) 962-8898

This theatre was constructed in the 1920s about the same time as its larger cousins, the Pantages, Palace, and Warner Pacific theatres. But this place included several luxury apartments in addition to a large hall used for stage plays, movie showing, and gala Hollywood parties with up to 500 guests. Today, the security apartments are not accessible to uninvited visitors. In 1971, the famous Knickerbocker bar was closed and sealed due to frequent poltergeist activity. In 1993 a portion of the building was opened as the All Star Theatre Café and Speakeasy. This café preserves some of the Hollywood atmosphere for which this landmark building was known.

There are plenty of ghosts here as a result of several tragic events. When Elvis stayed here, he was inspired to write "Heartbreak Hotel." He must have picked up on the sad vibes. In 1948, filmmaker D. W. Griffith suffered severe chest pain as he entered the building. He dropped dead under the chandelier in the lobby. William Frawley, who played Fred on the *I Love Lucy* show, never made it in the front door. He collapsed and died on the sidewalk. A celebrity dress designer named Irene killed herself after her affair with Gary Cooper ended. She left a note in an upstairs bathroom and jumped out the window. Unfortunately, her body landed on the grand entry roof and was not found for days.

Other events that occurred here could have created hauntings or the lingering presence of spiritual entities. Bess Houdini conducted séances from 1926 to 1936 on the anniversary of Harry's death. She received secret code words from his spirit, or so it is rumored. Marilyn Monroe and Joe DiMaggio used to meet in secret in the kitchen to avoid the press, and problems with their other relationships. Later, they spent their honeymoon in one of the elegant suites. Silent screen star Rudolph Valentino used to meet women at the bar, then take them upstairs for a night of sex.

Several visitors to the café have noticed the tall man who stands next to the serving counter. Dressed in black, he ignores the people around him, but vanishes when spoken to. Many have reported the apparition of Marilyn Monroe walking through the café. Several women have run out of the lady's restroom after hearing knocks on the wall, seeing a shorthaired woman in the mirror, or sensing a creepy feeling of being watched.

Famed ghost hunter Richard Senate investigated this place for several TV programs presented on Discovery and the History and Travel Channels. Working with a psychic, he found the spirits of movie star Fannie Farmer, D. W. Griffith, and a former bell captain of the hotel. Others have sensed the presence of a woman who had several encounters with Rudolph Valentino.

THE GHOST SINGER

Pantages Theatre
6233 Hollywood Boulevard
Hollywood 90028-1770
(323) 468-1770

Alexander Pantages opened this magnificent art-deco theatre on June 4, 1930, as a monument to his career in the entertainment industry. This opulent theatre in the heart of Hollywood presented movies, vaudeville acts, concerts, newsreels, and cartoons. In the 1950s, the Pantages hosted the Oscars, then continued as a first-class movie house until 1967, when it closed for refurbishing. The Pantages reopened in 1969 with several movie premieres only to close again in 1977 for major upgrades to the stage and sound and lighting systems. The Pantages reopened in art-deco splendor as the finest legitimate theatre in California. Today, it hosts Broadway touring companies and the best of local performers.

In 1932, during the performance of a musical, a young woman

The ghosts of Alexander Pantages and a female singer haunt the mezzanine and first-floor aisles of this Hollywood landmark.

died in the mezzanine, under mysterious circumstances. According to Hollywood legend, she was an aspiring actress who was depressed after several unsuccessful auditions. Early in 1990, after vandals damaged part of the balcony near her death site, the woman began performing at the Pantages Theatre. Several people heard her singing popular show tunes in the mezzanine. Housekeeping staff heard her voice in the mornings, theatre staff heard her late in the afternoon, and theatre patrons heard her singing in the evenings. As years passed, this ghost sang longer and louder. In 1994, her voice was picked up by nearby stage microphones as she sang along with the cast of a musical play.

The break-in by vandals that occurred in 1990 aroused other ghosts. In the second-floor offices, the apparition of a tall man has been seen. He opens and closes desk drawers, turns doorknobs, and creates intense cold spots. Ghost hunters believe this is the ghost of a former owner, Howard Hughes. On the main floor of the theatre, invisible hands assisted a wardrobe lady as she made her way up the aisle. The lights had been turned off and the aisle safety lights had failed, leaving her stumbling about in complete darkness. In telling her story, she believed her guide was none other than the ghost of Alexander Pantages.

GHOSTLY GUESTS

Hollywood Roosevelt Hotel
7000 Hollywood Boulevard
Hollywood 90028
(213) 466-7000
www.hollywoodroosevelt.com

Built by stars Douglas Fairbanks and Mary Pickford, this Hollywood icon opened in 1927 and became a landmark by hosting the first Academy Awards banquet. Instantly, the Roosevelt Hotel became the foremost gathering place in town for stars and movie moguls. It is still a great place for star gazing, whether the stars are alive or dead. Ghost hunters and psychic investigators have detected the presence of Marilyn Monroe and Ethel Merman near the pool,

The ghosts of several stars from Hollywood's golden era still hang out at the famous Roosevelt Hotel.

Errol Flynn and Betty Grable in the Blossom Room, and Carmen Miranda, Humphrey Bogart, and Charles Laughton at the poolside Tropicana Bar.

Upstairs, the ghost of Montgomery Clift haunts the ninth-floor corridor and room 928. Clift stayed in 928 for three months while filming the Academy Award-winning *From Here to Eternity.* Hotel maids have experienced his ghost as a cold breeze that passes them in the hall. Others have seen his apparition pacing the corridor, practicing his lines, or rehearsing his trumpet. Psychic Peter James spent a night in 928 but he was not alone. Around 2:00 A.M. James was a wakened by the weight of a man lying on top of him. A few hours later, the apparition appeared in a bedside chair. The ghost watched James for nearly 30 minutes before vanishing. Others who have stayed in this room have felt the ghost's touch and experienced his pranks. His playful nature is in contrast to the anger sensed by Peter James.

Reflections of dead guests have been seen in several mirrors throughout the hotel. A mirror that once graced a room used by Marilyn Monroe reflects her image and gives psychically sensitive viewers a sense of sadness. This mirror now hangs in the lower elevator foyer.

In the Blossom Room, a man dressed in a white suit stands next to the piano. He looks quite real, but vanishes when approached. Piano music played by a most talented musician has been heard in this room. Also in this room, a cold column of air has been detected. Psychic investigation suggests this is the ghost of a man in an anxious state dressed in a tuxedo. There is speculation that he is an Academy Award nominee awaiting the opening of the envelope in 1928.

Nearly solid apparitions have been seen by security staff, hotel management, and guests at the pool, at the ballroom mezzanine, in the bar, and on almost every floor. For instance, Carole Lombard's ghost has been seen on the twelfth floor near a room she often shared with Clark Gable. A five-year-old girl named Caroline skips through the lobby looking for her mother. On the third floor, hotel engineers have spotted a ghostly man wearing a white suit and 1920s footwear.

NIGHTCLUB GHOSTS

The Comedy Store (formerly Ciro's nightclub)
8433 Sunset Boulevard
West Hollywood 90069-1909
(323) 656-6225

Ciro's was one of the hot spots on Hollywood's famous Sunset Strip. Built in the late 1930s, this nightclub was the place where Hollywood stars and other famous people went for drinks, dancing, and entertainment in the 1940s and '50s. Stars such as Robert Taylor, Barbara Stanwyck, Frank Sinatra, Humphrey Bogart, Rock Hudson, and Clark Gable were regulars. Beyond the Hollywood glitter, mobsters such as Mickey Cohen moved in the shadows. Legend tells us that Cohen had his fingers in the business and took a piece of the

Ciro's Comedy Club, now the Comedy Store, was the scene of gangster activity in the 1930s and 1949s. Several big stars got their start here.

receipts each week. When things didn't go right, he took a pound of flesh too. Many of the ghosts residing at today's Comedy Store were victims of the mobster's wrath. Ghost investigators Laurie Jacobsen and Dr. Barry Taff believe that at least five ghosts are bound here.

In the basement, where mobsters tortured or murdered people who failed to meet their demands, psychic investigator Dr. Barry Taff experienced agonizing pain in his legs. He believes he picked up the emotional imprint of an unfortunate fellow whose legs were broken by Cohen's men. Growling sounds have also been heard at this location. Security staff have seen a padlocked gate bend outward as if some super-strong force were pushing against it. A tall black ghost has been seen here as well. Laurie Jacobsen described this entity as evil and malevolent. This may be the ghost of a hit man.

In a room identified as the original showroom of Ciro's nightclub, three men dressed in 1940s suits were observed standing in the shadows as a Haunted Hollywood TV program was filmed. Some thought they were actors dressed in period costume for the program. But when Dr. Taff approached them, they vanished.

Late at night, while locking up, workers have seen chairs slide across the stage and found glassware arranged on tables that were cleaned off for the night. During performances, stage staff have heard ghosts make comments about comedians. One comic, Sam Kinison, interrupted his performance and challenged a distracting ghost to show himself. At that moment, all the lights in the building went out.

In the kitchen area and second-floor offices, a man in a brown leather bomber jacket moves about. He has been seen cowering in dark corners and dashing from one room to the next. Witnesses say the man appears terrified and is hiding from mobsters. Many believe he is the ghost of one of Cohen's victims.

Today, the old nightclub runs hot as a top comedy venue in Hollywood. Stars Jim Carrey, Richard Pryor, and David Letterman got their start here, and new talent is showcased each week. Robin Williams, Whoopi Goldberg, Steve Martin, Garry Shandling, and Pauly Shore are Comedy Store alumni who stop by when they are in town. An evening at this place can be very lively even if you hang out with a dead person.

ALBERT, THE PLAYHOUSE GHOST

Conejo Players Theatre
351 South Moorpark Road
Thousand Oaks 91361
(805) 495-3715
www.conejoplayers.org

Most community theatre groups have dedicated staff, reliable supporters, a stable of gifted actors, and generous patrons, but few include a ghost as a lifetime member of the theatre management committee. Some people question whether the term "lifetime" can be applied to Albert's status, because he is quite dead.

Albert resides at the Conejo Valley Players Theatre fully dedicating himself to the company. He is very active, expressing his criticism of performances by stomping his feet in the aisles, relocating props to more artistic positions (or hiding them), or removing personal items from actors, such as cell phones and jewelry, that should not be seen on stage. Albert has been heard warning actors that they are about to step offstage into the footlights, tumble off a raised platform, or grab a loose hand railing.

For many years, Albert was simply known as the "theatre ghost." One night, an actor scribbled a note before leaving the theatre. "Mr. Ghost, what is your name?" The next day, "Albert" was found written on a wall near the note. But this ghost has revealed more than his name. A group photograph taken on the steps of the theatre was found to include a face no one could identify. Many believe the face is Albert's. This ghost is so beloved by Conejo Players that a theatre seat was sponsored in his name. A plaque on the armrest affirms that "Albert the Ghost" is a member of theatre's community of supporters.

The good feelings associated with this ghost's presence are in contrast to his probable history. Many years before the Conejo Players Theatre was constructed, the company used a nearby church for performances. This church—Missionary Baptist Church—was a rebuilt barn. During a visit to the site, psychic Sybil Leek sensed that a young man had been stabbed to death in the barn. Other psychics confirmed awareness of violence, particularly in the attic.

The Conejo Players first became aware of a ghost when they used this building for performances. His antics were playful but not particularly frightening or menacing. Soon after moving to the new theatre, the familiar paranormal activity continued, suggesting to many that the ghost of the old barn had moved on to new quarters with the theatre company.

BORDELLO GHOST

Four Oaks Restaurant
2181 North Beverly Glen Boulevard
Bell Air 90077
(310) 470-2265

In the 1880s, travel between the city of Los Angeles and San Fernando Valley ranches was not easy. In fact, it was often a dusty, hot, sweaty affair for passengers as well as the horses that pulled coaches up the winding road through Beverly Glen Canyon. The trip was so taxing that an inn and café were built midway through the canyon at a spot lush with shade trees and grass fed by several springs. Travelers rested and dined while horse teams were changed. The place became known as the Four Oaks Inn and Café because of a huge oak tree nearby that was formed from four separate tree trunks.

Business boomed until the 1920s, when alternative roads and automobiles provided faster and more comfortable means of traveling between the valley and L.A. After 40 years, the Four Oaks Inn and Café lost its fine reputation and classy appearance when the inn became a speakeasy, offering bootleg liquor in the bar and full-service bordello on the second floor. No doubt, the roaring '20s brought unsavory characters from the nearby city, criminals, college men bent on a riotous night of drinking, and others looking for a fight. Any one of these types might have lost his life here. Added to that, prostitutes who worked there must have included desperate women who suffered terrible treatment at the hands of customers, pimps, or bosses.

This kind of history makes it difficult to identify the mysterious figure that appears at the Four Oaks. The ghost has been described as a large, glowing apparition that hovers near the fireplace in the dining room or in the bar. It has been seen by many but no one can give a clear description of the ghost's features or determine if it is a man or woman. A former owner once saw this ghost throw open a door and enter his upstairs apartment. This ghost radiated light and stayed quite a while in spite of the owner's screaming, "Go away! Go away! You don't belong here!"

Ghost hunters speculate about the possibility that the bordello ghost at Four Oaks has something do to with a murder that occurred down the road. In another 1880s vintage roadhouse, a husband found his wife in bed with her lover. In a rage, the husband cut off the man's head with a scythe, spraying blood all over the bed and the terrified wife. He was later executed for the murder while the unfaithful wife inherited his fortune. It is likely that she moved on to a luxurious lifestyle in a higher social strata. Her husband and lover, however, are still in Beverly Glen Canyon, searching for each other.

The headless man, dressed in his favorite yellow opera cape and black-tie ensemble, has been seen on the roadside near the abandoned roadhouse in which he was murdered. He seems to be quite friendly. In the 1970s, occupants of the building described him as comforting, sympathetic, and playful. He even went for rides in a woman's car but got out before reaching the modern city. This headless ghost, clad in his yellow cape, has been seen outside the Four Oaks as well. The glowing ghost that appears inside the restaurant can be noisy and frightening. He may be the jealous husband, still searching for the man who destroyed his happy home.

The old roadhouse is no longer occupied. It sits on the 1400 block of North Beverly Glen Boulevard. The Four Oaks Restaurant is a four-star establishment that offers world-class cuisine, service, and atmosphere that attracts entertainers, sports stars, and others in the movie industry.

GHOST OF ORSON WELLES

Sweet Lady Jane Bakery and Restaurant
8360 Melrose Avenue
Los Angeles 90069
(323) 653-3771
www.sweetladyjane.com

Oscar-winning director-actor-producer Orson Welles (1915-85)

The ghost of director-writer Orson Welles still visits Sweet Lady Jane's Hollywood café.

once declared, "I began at the top and have been making my way down ever since." At the age of 26, in 1941, he reached his zenith with *Citizen Kane* and earned an Oscar for best script. By 1980, his spectacular career had lost much of its luster. Welles became a frequent guest on TV talk shows and a spokesman in various TV commercials. His status in the film industry fell to a level that was personally disappointing and surprising to his many fans, but Orson Welles was still one of the most recognizable personalities in the business. Seeking simple comforts in his later years, he took long walks throughout Hollywood, stopping frequently at a favorite restaurant now called Sweet Lady Jane.

This cozy cafe on Melrose Avenue is known for pastries that range from the simplest scones to complex wedding cakes. In Welles' day, it was a modest coffee shop known by another name. Its comforts were so endearing that Orson still drops by the upscale shop 20 years after his death. Patrons and staff report his partial apparition, complete with his signature black cape, sitting in his favorite booth. The odors of his favorite cigars and brandy have been detected as well, in spite of rules prohibiting smoking and alcoholic beverages. Some people have heard Orson's distinctive voice ordering more brandy.

Skeptics and detractors claim that Welles' ghost does not visit Sweet Lady Jane. They recount the story told years ago about how a reporter disguised himself as Orson Welles and walked past the window, surprising patrons who were convinced they had seen a ghost. But many staff and regular customers here tell of odors and partial apparitions that could not be Hollywood special effects.

PHANTOMS OF GRIFFITH PARK

4730 Crystal Springs Drive
Los Angeles 90027
(323) 913-4688

This 4,000-acre urban park is haunted by several phantoms, including a Yankee horseman, a bearded man who travels briskly on foot, a group of mission Indians who appears to be on the run, a Mexican outlaw, a Spanish don, and Col. G. J. Griffith on horseback.

Foremost of these is the ghost of Dona Petranilla Feliz. She appears as a pale, partial apparition of a short Hispanic woman dressed in a flowing white gown. This ghost walks the hillsides that were, at one time, her birthright.

In 1863, Dona Petranilla's father—Don Feliz—died of smallpox. In order to secure the future of his great Rancho Los Feliz, he willed the property to his best friend, Don Antonio Colonel with the expectation that it would be managed for the benefit of his blind 16-year-old daughter. Don Antonio was charged with insuring the comfort and financial security of helpless Dona Petranilla. Once the property became his legal domain, however, Don Antonio ruled the rancho as his own, leaving Dona Petranilla to fend for herself.

Enraged, she cursed the land and her father for leaving her birthright in the hands of such an unscrupulous man. "This is what I hurl on your head," she screamed at Don Antonio. "Your falsity shall be your ruin. Misfortune, crime, and death shall follow those who covet these remains."

From that day onward, most of the people involved in the management or ownership of Rancho Los Feliz suffered some terrible calamity. The probate judge who upheld Don Antonio's position in certain disputes suddenly dropped dead. A lawyer who administered the estate was shot in a bar.

There were so many disasters that Don Antonio finally sold the land to Leon Baldwin. Baldwin immediately starting losing money on expensive improvements that failed to pay off. One night, a bandit accosted him on the property, took his wallet, and killed him. Baldwin's ghost may be seen as a bearded man who wanders the park's trails on foot, having lost his horse to the bandit.

In 1884, Col. Griffith J. Griffith acquired the land, but he also had many difficulties, including water sources that dried up, droughts, fires, and other disasters. That same year, a violent storm swept across the L.A. basin, stripping away the vegetation from the rancho and killing much of the livestock. During the storm, several people saw the ghost of Dona Petranilla drifting about, renewing her curse. Griffith donated most of the land to the City of Los Angeles on December 16, 1896. The spin was that the land was a Christmas gift to the city to create a place of rest and recreation for the masses. The truth is that Griffith was desperate to get rid of the haunted grounds, but could find no buyer. Donating the cursed land didn't help him escape the wrath of Dona Petranilla though. Griffith developed some kind of mental disorder and tried to kill his wife. He spent a few years in San Quentin for that offense but died in Los Angeles on July 7, 1919.

Today, Griffith Park is the kind of urban paradise Colonel Griffith envisioned. The Greek theatre, observatory and planetarium, equestrian center, miles of riding trails, train park, and other attractions are surrounded by thousands of acres of natural terrain preserved for the enjoyment of the general public. The ghosts who roam these acres seem unaware of modern developments. They remain here, tied to the land by the curse of Dona Petranilla that brought them ruin.

GHOST OF CHIEF BUFFALO CHILD LONG LANCE

Los Angeles County Arboretum
301 North Baldwin Avenue
Arcadia 91006
(626) 821-3222
www.arboretum.org/

In the late 1920s, few movie roles were available to black men. But actors who could portray Indians were in demand, especially if they looked and spoke in ways that convinced audiences they were real Native Americans. Recognizing a way to achieve his dream of being in the movies, one clever African-American developed the right accent and mannerisms and soon found work. By 1931, Chief Buffalo Child Long Lance, as he called himself, had appeared in several movies with speaking roles. The "chief" was so convincing that he also worked as a technical consultant and writer to add authenticity to Indian story lines. His success opened many doors in Hollywood, including the privilege of residing in the 1885 Queen Anne Cottage on the grounds of theatre magnate Lucky Baldwin's Santa Anita Rancho.

For a few years, Chief Long Lance enjoyed the lifestyle of a minor movie star. However, in 1932, a reporter for the *Los Angeles Times*, acting on the suspicions of real Indians who worked with Long Lance, began snooping around. When the reporter confronted the chief with a number of allegations, the actor knew he was about to be revealed as a fraud. The humiliation would be too much for a man who was so desperate for work in the movies that he would deny his race and impersonate another. One night, in the solitude of the ornate Queen Anne Cottage parlor, Long Lance shot himself in the head. He fell to the floor and died, surrounded by opulence and luxury that he could have never achieved without his deception.

Perhaps death did not free the chief from his humiliation or guilt, or his dream of a big role in a major film, because his ghost still paces the parlor floor as if he is memorizing his lines. Staff of the Queen Anne Cottage—now the showpiece of the Los Angeles County Arboretum and Botanic Garden—have seen the apparition of Chief Long Lance. He is dressed in a tan-colored shirt and his hair is braided. He passes from one side of the room to the other, then turns and crosses back. Cast and crew of the television series *Fantasy Island,* including producer Aaron Spelling, saw this ghost many times. The cottage was used in the series as the residence of Mr. Roarke, played by Ricardo Montalban. TV buffs may remember Roarke's assistant, Mr. Tatto, opening the show from the tower by calling out, "De plane, de plane!"

Baldwin's cottage is not the only place in the arboretum that is familiar to visitors. The lake—also known as a lagoon, cienega, or sag pond—has been used as an outdoor set for several movies. Bob Hope, Bing Crosby, and Dorothy Lamour filmed *Road to Singapore* here in 1939. Alex Haley's TV minseries *Roots II* used the lake as an African river frequented by Kunta Kinte. More recently, Jennifer Lopez and Jon Voight, in *Anaconda,* battled a giant South American snake here.

Sites around the lake have been investigated by ghost hunters searching for spirits of Gabrielino Indians who were removed from their homes and pressed into labor at nearby Mission San Gabriel in the 1770s. Also, the ghost of Elias Jackson "Lucky" Baldwin is believed to appear in the Hugo Reid Adobe, creating cold spots and unexplainable gusts of air.

GHOST OF ALBERT WORKMAN

Shadow Ranch Park
22633 Vanowen Street
Canoga Park 91307
(818) 883-9370

When Albert Workman arrived in Southern California from his native Australia in the late 1850s, he found a land ripe with possibilities. Albert was smart enough to realize that food was the foundation of virtually every human enterprise and the future of the industrious Californians would depend on a plentiful local source. With a track record of agricultural success in arid Australia, Albert landed a job as superintendent of a huge San Fernando Valley wheat farm. The business was so successful that he was able to purchase the 9,000-acre ranch in 1869. Soon he added another 4,000 acres and became one of the largest wheat suppliers in Southern California. At one time, his ranch included 70 barns, a thousand head of cattle, and hundreds of workers. Albert imported eucalyptus trees from Australia in the 1870s and planted them at various sites near the house. These trees are believed to be the forerunners of all eucalyptus in Southern California. The shadows cast by these tall, rapid-growing trees inspired the name for Workman's Shadow Ranch.

Workman's family lived in a huge ranch house that combined adobe style with contemporary American redwood construction. It included a dining room that served meals to 70 workers in one sitting, offices, a private family dining room, kitchens, and several bedrooms. The house stands today as the focal point of the 13-acre Shadow Ranch Park.

After Albert's death, his children married and moved away, selling off pieces of the ranch to pay for a new start elsewhere. Eventually, the ranch was reduced to a 13-acre plot that became a park within the blossoming San Fernando Valley community of Canoga Park. Little is left of Workman's grand domain with the exception of his ranch house. And this is something with which he refuses to part. His ghost stands watch here, pacing the halls and rooms of the second floor, walking the stairs, and staring out the windows at visitors.

Staff and visitors have seen Workman's partial apparition floating through the house. He is a quiet ghost, but he sometimes creates the sound of heavy boots on wooden floors and stairs. From the outside, visitors to Shadow Ranch Park have seen an old man wearing a weathered straw hat gazing out the second-floor windows. At night, the soft glow of candlelight has been seen in the windows of the second-floor east rooms.

GHOST OF VICTOR KILIAN AND THE BACKSTAGE GHOST

Grauman's Chinese Theatre
6925 Hollywood Boulevard
Hollywood 90028
(323) 464-8111

Victor Kilian was one of the little people in Hollywood. His face was familiar and his voice distinctive, but most people who met him could not quite place him. His Irish character came through at times but he could take on almost any accent when needed. Victor Kilian was familiar because he appeared in nearly 150 movies. He was not a stand-in or an extra. He had plenty of speaking roles but never became a star. Late in his career, he switched to TV and appeared in the offbeat, late-night comedy series *Mary Hartman, Mary Hartman.*

In 1976, Kilian's career was history but he couldn't leave Hollywood. He rented a nice apartment at 6500 Yucca Street and hung out at bars, theatres, and cafés, rubbing elbows with other Hollywood old-timers. One night, Victor met a fellow in a bar near his apartment. They hit it off, talking about the old days, the great stars, and the tyrannical directors. After last call at the bar, the two men went to Victor's apartment to continue their reminiscences. It was there that something went wrong.

Victor had little money, little jewelry, and no keepsakes of significant value. But something triggered violence in the visitor. The next morning, Victor's body was found severely beaten about the head, neck, and torso. The visitor had disappeared without a trace.

The only clue to the murder is that it might have had something

The ghost of murder victim Victor Killian has been seen pacing the sidewalk in front of this Hollywood icon theatre.

to do with the Chinese Theatre. The story goes that Victor Kilian's ghost revealed that clue, for he wanders the sidewalk in front of the famous 1927 theatre built by Sid Grauman. Psychic investigation revealed that Victor Kilian is looking for the man who murdered him. The obvious conclusion is that the murderer frequented the theatre, worked there, or passed by often.

It is interesting to add that the Chinese Theatre has a ghost too. He is known as the "backstage ghost" because sightings occur behind the screen near the ropes that control the main curtain. This ghost also roams the dressing rooms, disrupting anyone working there. The backstage ghost is more than a trickster. He creates in people a creepy feeling of being watched. He moves tools and props, hides things, plays with light switches, disturbs electrical equipment, and slams doors. If this fellow murdered Victor Kilian, he might be nervous about the other ghost who waits for him in front of Grauman's Chinese Theatre.

GHOST OF MARILYN MONROE

Corridor of Memories, Crypt #24
Westwood Village Memorial Park
1218 Glendon Avenue
Los Angeles 90024
(310) 474-1579

Her death was tragic and senseless, leaving the entire country wondering how this could have happened to such a famous lady. But there was doubt that the sex kitten of the '60s, Marilyn Monroe, was dead. Several watched late at night on August 5, 1962, as her body was carried from her home at 12305 Fifth Helena Drive in Brentwood. She died at the age of 36 after a brief, but spectacular career as a star in more than 30 films. Marilyn was also a veteran of three marriages, one of these to baseball great Joe DiMaggio.

Marilyn was born Norma Jean Mortenson on June 1, 1926, in Los Angeles. She later changed her last name to Baker, her mother's maiden name, when she discovered that her father's identity was uncertain. After signing a contract with Twentieth Century Fox Studios, Norma

The crypt of Marilyn Monroe attracts visitors trying to contact her spirit.

Jean became Marilyn Monroe. She had minor roles in several movies before becoming a star in *Bus Stop* (1956). Her success at playing the sexy, voluptuous blonde in *Some Like It Hot* (1959) typecast her for years. Marilyn did not achieve recognition as a serious actress until 1961, when she starred with Clark Gable in *The Misfits.*

The story goes that friends, including her personal physician, Dr. Ralph Greenson, found Marilyn in her bedroom, dead or close to it. Her death was ruled a suicide by an overdose of the drug Nembutal. The L.A. County coroner, Thomas Noguchi, was unable to find traces of this drug in her stomach or intestines, however.

There is some evidence and a lot of speculation that Marilyn's death was not a suicide. In his book *L.A. Exposed,* Paul Young presents a number of possibilities. These include an attempt by Mafioso to expose Robert Kennedy's alleged affair with the actress and to destroy his political career by implicating him in her death. Another possibility is that J. Edgar Hoover was behind her death because he hated both Robert and John Kennedy, and they had both had sexual encounters with Marilyn. There is even speculation that Robert Kennedy had a direct hand in her death and that he was present at her home with Dr. Greenson the night she died. The truth will probably never be known, adding to the mystique of Marilyn's life and death.

Various psychics claim to have made contact with the screen star. Many report that she insists her death was not a suicide. Marilyn's ghost has been reported in front of her Brentwood home. Psychic Anton La Vey and writer Bob Slatzer reported seeing her nearly solid image near the sidewalk. It is interesting to note that when Marilyn was first removed from the house, she was still alive. She died in an ambulance in front of her house or nearby on San Vicente Boulevard while on the way to the hospital. One story says that her body was returned to the house by order of Kennedy family member Peter Lawford to allow incriminating evidence to be removed or altered. Later, a coroner carried her corpse away. The appearance of Marilyn's ghost outside the house has been interpreted as a sign that she did not die in her bedroom as reported by the press.

Marilyn's 1954 marriage to Joe DiMaggio ended after only nine months, but his love for her never failed. After her death, Joe had red roses delivered to Marilyn's crypt twice each week for 20 years. That service has long since ended, but other admirers often leave flowers and other items. Several ghost hunters have seen Marilyn's apparition hovering near her grave. She appears as a misty cloud, perhaps waiting for roses to be delivered.

GHOSTS OF THE BIG STARS

Hollywood Forever Cemetery
6000 Santa Monica Boulevard
Hollywood 90038
(323) 469-1181
www.hollywoodforever.com

In 1899, Hollywood Memorial Park opened its doors and quickly became the preferred resting place for movie stars, movie moguls, and other big-name entertainers. During the wild times of the 1920s, the Depression of the 1930s, and the somber World War II years, its prestige and level of maintenance fluctuated vastly, reaching a low point in the 1980s. At times, various scandals plagued its managers, culminating in a bankruptcy in the 1990s. New backers restored the beauty and grandeur of the grounds, headstones, and mausoleum befitting the graves of some of America's greatest stars such as Douglas Fairbanks, Tyrone Power, John Huston, Mel Blanc, Peter Lorre, Marian Davies, Victor Fleming, and producer Cecil B. DeMille. In addition, gangsters such as Bugsy Siegel are buried here. Renamed Hollywood Forever Cemetery, this graveyard is a Mecca for film buffs, history nuts, and ghost hunters.

One of the best spots for ghost hunting here is at crypt number 1205 in the Cathedral Mausoleum. The great silent-film star Rudolph Valentino rests here. This was supposed to be a temporary stop for the dashing actor, who died at age 31, but his custom-designed crypt was never completed. He was laid to rest in 1926 and mourned by women all over the world. One of them was so distraught over his death, she visited his grave once each week wearing traditional black. Her devotion to the romantic film star was so strong that her own death has not stopped her from visiting Rudy.

The apparition of a lady dressed in black, complete with black veil over her face, has been seen kneeling in front of crypt 1205. Several apparitions are seen near this crypt on August 23, the anniversary of Rudy's death.

In the lobby of the Abbey of the Psalms mausoleum, an apparition identified as Clifton Webb has been seen. Known for the fastidious tendencies he used in portraying his on-screen characters, Webb died in October 1966. Days before his death, Webb confided in psychic Kenny Kingston that he had seen the ghost of his dear friend, actress and stage-performer Grace Moore, in his house. He added that he intended to remain at his Rexford Drive home and visit his favorite spots in Hollywood even after his death. Apparently, this includes the cemetery where he was interred.

At the grave of silent-film star Virginia Rappe, embodied sobbing is often heard. Ghost hunters believe this is Virginia's ghost lamenting the terrible end of a sad, short life in 1921. Many people believe that the actress died as a result of a drunken, sexual brawl at the St. Francis Hotel in San Francisco with 300-pound Fatty Arbuckle. In fact, others attending this wild Labor Day weekend party, including Virginia's friend Maude Delmont, testified in court that Arbuckle ruptured Virginia's bladder with his crushing weight during sex or penetrated her with a Coke bottle or champagne bottle. Writer Paul Young discounts this story in his book *L.A. Exposed.* He claims Virginia was in San Francisco for her sixth abortion, which she underwent just a day or two prior to Arbuckle's wild party. It is likely that she was injured internally during the procedure, performed by a Dr. Rumwell, and became acutely ill with peritonitis while visiting Maude Delmont and other friends at the St. Francis Hotel. Arbuckle was exonerated and the scandal grew to include Paramount Studios president, Adolph Zukor, and San Francisco D.A., Matthew Brady. In any event, it appears that Virginia's ghost still feels the pain of her tragic life and early death. She stands at her grave, among other Hollywood legends, sobbing.

Ghostly apparitions, cold spots, icy breezes, thickened atmosphere, shadows, and disembodied voices singing, crying, and sobbing have been experienced at numerous grave sites of the rich, famous, and infamous.

On summer weekends, Hollywood Forever Cemetery stages a unique screening of old movies that attracts hundreds of movie buffs and others who hope to get in touch with personalities from the golden age of film. Visitors spread blankets among grave markers, lay out gourmet picnic dinners, pour the Chardonnay, and relax under the stars—and over the stars—while viewing a classic movie projected onto the walls of the mausoleum. The romantic atmosphere can turn a bit spooky, creating a unique Hollywood experience.

INTERSECTION APPARITIONS

North Sierra Bonita Avenue at Hollywood Boulevard
Hollywood 90046

This is a strange and curious place. North Sierra Bonita Avenue and Hollywood Boulevard are modern streets full of traffic almost anytime of day or evening. When standing on the corner, it is hard to imagine that a haunting may occur here because there is a definite lack of peace and quiet, something ghosts seem to prefer. Attempts to meditate and get in touch with vibrations of the environment are often interrupted by noisy cars or trucks. But patience pays off.

Many apparitions have been seen here. Noted expert of the paranormal Dennis William Hauck described an accident in which a driver ran off the street and hit a tree in order to avoid hitting a covered wagon as it passed through the intersection. Others have reported apparitions of Indians in the streets, on foot and on horseback, and arrows flying through the air. Many have seen Mexican bandits on horseback here as well as other early Californians in small wagons. These apparitions look quite solid, appear out of nowhere, and then fade away.

There is no apparent reason why this particular intersection should be such a haunted site, but there is speculation that nearby Wattles Garden Park and Runyon Canyon Park may have something to do with it. These open space areas, which have escaped development, may have a spiritual history that preserves the land. Places such as these should be investigated as possible Indian burial grounds, sites of early pioneer disasters, or some other cataclysmic event that created strong emotional imprints on the environment.

Famed San Diego ghost hunter John Lamb offers another interesting observation. In his book *San Diego Specters,* Lamb notes that natural water sources such as springs are often associated with hauntings and speculates that they may serve as conduits for spirits visiting our world from the other side. It would be interesting to search Wattles Garden and Runyon Canyon parks for springs or creeks that flow toward the intersection of North Sierra Bonita Avenue and Hollywood Boulevard.

GHOSTS OF THE STARS AT FOREST LAWN

Forest Lawn Memorial Park
1712 South Glendale Avenue
Glendale 91205
(323) 254-3131

This cemetery is believed to be the final resting place for more Hollywood stars and other notables than any other graveyard in the world. The grounds cover more than 300 acres decorated with sculptures, courts, lakes, fountains, and several English-style chapels. The management does not welcome sightseers, movie buffs, or ghost hunters. Therefore, visitors should be unobtrusive and respectful of the management staff and people interred here.

It may be useful to obtain a guidebook for this cemetery or visit www.seeing-stars.com/buried2/ForestLawnGlendale.shtml. Also, do a little research to identify a star whose ghost you hunt. You may learn of unique characteristics that can help you identify the spirit behind paranormal activity. There are plenty of stars to investigate, including W. C. Fields, Sammy Davis, Jr., Red Skelton, Nat King Cole, George Burns, Humphrey Bogart, Carole Lombard, Jean Harlow, Jimmy Stewart, Spencer Tracy, Clark Gable, Dorothy Dandridge, the Marx brothers, Alan Ladd, and Jack Carson. Industry greats Walt Disney, David O. Selznick, Irving Thalberg, and Sid Grauman are here too.

In the Court of Freedom, comedian George Burns (1896-1996) rests in tomb #203602 with his wife, Gracie Allen. In life, George was never without his trademark cigar. Some ghost hunters have detected the odor of a cigar close to this tomb. The odor occupies a small space of about one cubic foot without evidence that it was carried in by a breeze.

In this area, on the south wall, are the tombs of Alan Ladd (#203582, 1913-64), Nat King Cole (#203692, 1919-65), Jeanette MacDonald (#203642, 1903-65), and Clara Bow (#203484, 1905-65). Soft, unintelligible voices have been heard, as if ghosts are whispering to each other.

In the Great Mausoleum, actress Jean Harlow (1911-37) rests, sort of. Jean was ranked with Marilyn Monroe as a Hollywood sex symbol. Her blond bombshell persona and "live fast, die young" lifestyle made her a huge star but she died suddenly, at age 26, of cerebral edema due to kidney failure. In her short life, Jean was married three times. Her second husband, Paul Bern, shot himself in the head on September 5, 1932, in Jean's house at 9820 Easton Drive, Beverly Hills. At her gravesite, soft sobbing has been heard. Psychic investigation revealed a sense of bewilderment and anger.

Intense paranormal sensations have been experienced at the gravesite shared by Clark Gable and Carole Lombard. Lombard (1908-42) died in a tragic plane crash while returning from a war bond drive. An odd sense of confusion and anger has been detected at the grave of "Superman" George Reeves. Reeves shot himself on June 16, 1958. Much later, information was uncovered that suggests he was murdered by mobster Eddie Mannix. At the grave of Playmate of the Year 1980, Dorothy Stratten, a partial apparition has been seen. It resembles a pale mist floating a few feet off the ground. Dorothy was killed at the age of 20 by her estranged husband, who then turned the gun on himself. Their turbulent marriage and tragic end was portrayed in the movie *Star 80*.

GHOSTS OF THE OBAN HOTEL

6364 Yucca Street
Hollywood 90028
(213) 466-0524

This graceful, aging hotel was built in the early 1930s to accommodate the flood of aspiring actors and actresses who descended upon Hollywood with dreams of stardom. In fact, quite a few stars spent a little time here, including Clark Gable, Fred MacMurray,

Marilyn Monroe, and Paul Newman. Band leaders such as Glenn Miller stayed here with their musicians awaiting the big break. Several Hollywood wannabes stayed here too. Some had to be content to work behind the scenes, as was props manager Charles Love.

Charlie Love worked on the set of several movies making sure props were in their places, managing details that made scenes look authentic. His aspirations to be an actor were only partly satisfied by working as a stunt double for star Harry Langdon. Hollywood legend tells us that Charlie had a big argument with someone at the studio, went on a drinking spree for a couple of days, then returned to his room at the Oban, wrote a suicide note addressed to Harry Langdon, and shot himself. His ghost has been there ever since his death on February 15, 1933.

Hotel Oban owners, staff, and patrons have detected Charlie's ghost on the stairs leading to the basement and in the basement itself. Charlie creates tremendous cold spots, the creepy feeling of being watched, and

The ghosts of Charlie Love and others have been found at the old Oban Hotel by professional ghost hunters.

a thickening of the air. At times, an apparition described as the shadow of a man without a distinct outline appears. Reports state that the figure changes color from black to rust. Ghost investigators Laurie Jacobsen and Marc Wanamaker reported that Love created a foul odor in the basement when they visited the site and inquired about his death. They interpret this terrible, nauseating odor as a sign that Charlie did not commit suicide but was murdered. Psychics investigating paranormal activity at this site also concluded that the ghost was a murder victim. It seems he remains at the Oban Hotel awaiting discovery of his murderer.

Psychic investigation also detected the ghost of a female on the second floor of the hotel. Ghost hunters learned that she stays close to the room in which she died because she cannot find her way to the hotel's main door.

The ghosts of two men, one of them a former owner of the Oban Hotel, have been found at the top of the stairs that lead to the basement. A man who owned the hotel in the '80s reported to ghost hunters that he was aware of a steady stream of spirits throughout the old hotel, most of them from the 1930s. He suggested that they were still waiting for that big break that would make them a Hollywood star.

THREE GHOSTS OF EL COMPADRE RESTAURANT

7408 Sunset Boulevard
Hollywood 90046-3404
(323) 874-7924

This modest, Spanish-style building has served as a bar and restaurant since it opened in the 1920s. That long track record is well deserved. The food and service are great. The atmosphere is relaxing, unless unsuspecting patrons run into the ghosts of El Compadre.

In the 1950s the restaurant was called Don Pepe's and most of the customers were streetwise young men and others who, it is said, lived in the shadow of the law. One night, the restaurant was robbed by three or four men wielding guns. Staff and customers ducked for cover as shots rang out, but two men were hit and died on the spot. The terror of this event was so sudden that the ghosts of these men

Ghosts of two men killed in a 1950s robbery still spend time at El Compadre Restaurant.

may not realize they are dead. They have been seen as two partial shadows, moving together near the present location of a piano. It is not known if a piano was located there at the time of the robbery and killing. One ghost hunter believes the men may have tried to hide behind a piano at this location during the robbery. Now, the two spirits may stay close to it for safety.

These ghosts have been described as floating shadows, sometimes appearing after cold spots are detected. They have been known to play with light switches, move objects around, and create the sound of footsteps. Disembodied voices have been reported too.

A third ghost has been detected at El Compadre Restaurant in the bar area. Also a male, this apparition has been seen near a large mirror, sometimes as a shadow in the mirror or a mist surrounding it. Staff and customers have reported a strange sensation of being watched or someone standing very close to them. It would be interesting to conduct a psychic investigation to determine if this ghost is associated with the robbery and killing that occurred here.

GHOSTS OF LOS ENCINOS

Los Encinos State Historic Park
16756 Moorpark Street
Encino 91436-1068
(818) 784-4849
www.los-encinos.org/

This state park is considered to be extremely haunted. Spirits have been sited at each of the three historic buildings, the Garnier House, the Reyes Hut, and the De La Osa Adobe.

In 1797, Francisco Reyes built a one-room stone structure that served as a blacksmith shop. The history of this structure is scanty, but psychic investigation of the site revealed evidence of at least one tragic event. Famed ghost hunter Richard Senate reported that an icy presence has been perceived here. One visitor felt that she could not get close to the building because of strong sensations of some terrible event. Psychic impressions have been reported of a murder in the stone building. It is told that the victim pleaded for his life, yet suffered a painful death. Today, emotions attached to this event linger at the site, giving visitors the impression that a ghost haunts the site seeking mercy. Voices whispering in Spanish have also been detected here.

In 1848, Don Vicente de La Osa built a large one-story adobe to house his family that included 14 children. Ghost hunters have encountered the spirit of a woman described as short with dark hair. Reports say she is very unhappy with issues pertaining to the ranch. Visitors to the large bedroom have felt a cold spot that gives the impression of a female presence.

The Eugene Garnier House was built of limestone in the 1870s in a style described as French provincial. The building was closed for many years, but has been recently renovated and is now open for visitors. During the time it was closed, ghost hunters saw the faces of three children gazing outward through the dirty windows. Psychic investigations uncovered the presence of a boy and two girls who died suddenly, by accident, either inside or close to the house. The ghosts of these children are waiting for someone to take them away to a safe place.

GHOST CARRIAGE OF LOOKOUT MOUNTAIN

Laurel Canyon Boulevard and Lookout Mountain Avenue
Los Angeles 90046

If you happen to be standing at the intersection of Lookout Mountain Avenue and Laurel Canyon Boulevard at the stroke of midnight, you had better watch out. A haunting occurs here that can be so frightening it has caused car accidents and left others with weak knees and a cold sweat.

The haunting is an apparition of a large black carriage pulled by two huge, white horses. The carriage appears from nowhere on Lookout Mountain Avenue, careens down the road with horses galloping at full speed, crosses Laurel Canyon Boulevard, then disappears. Witnesses seldom hear sounds but describe this apparition as huge, quite solid, and moving at great speed.

People familiar with the history of this area are not surprised by the appearance of a ghost carriage. One hundred fifty years ago, bands of outlaws roamed these hills preying on travelers, local ranchers, and prospectors. The bandit Tiburcio Vasquez and his men were most fearsome. They seldom left their victims with anything, including their lives. The havoc these outlaws created could have led to environmental imprints of emotional events such as the speeding black carriage of Lookout Mountain. The driver of this coach, scared to death, may have driven his horses at great speed down this road trying to outrun bandits. The appearance of the carriage here could mark the spot where the driver looked over his shoulder, only to find the bandits fast upon him.

It is interesting that many stories of hauntings and ghosts are told about this area. Some of Hollywood's early stars lived here, including Harry Houdini. The ruins of his mansion lie close to the intersection of Lookout Mountain Avenue and Laurel Canyon Boulevard. Nearby, Laurel Canyon Park has been the site of recent ghost hunts. Pale apparitions have been seen here preceded by spots of intense cold.

CHAPTER 3

Central Los Angeles and Eastside Communities

HALL OF JUSTICE HAUNTS

Los Angeles Hall of Justice
210 West Temple Street (at Spring Street and Broadway)
Los Angeles 90012

Over its 130-year history, the Los Angeles Hall of Justice has been the site of mob lynchings, official executions, gang wars, shootings, incarcerations of the rich and famous, trials of notorious killers, and a lucrative prostitution trade. This fantastic history creates great opportunities for ghost hunters. The building and surrounding grounds are known for ghostly apparitions, strange cold spots, orbs that appear in tourist's photographs, and the creepy feeling that the ghost of some famous criminal is only a step or two behind you.

Long before the present Hall of Justice was built, this site was part of the Wild West. In 1870, a shootout at high noon left four police officers dead or wounded. Among them was William C. Warren, the city's only police chief killed in the line of duty. On October 24, 1871, two Chinese *tongs* (gangs) staged a shootout here. An unfortunate white man was caught in the crossfire and wounded. The enraged citizenry, including whites and Latinos, raided the nearby Chinese ghetto, killing 18 gang members. Some of these fellows were hanged on a tree that stood on the current site of the main entrance to the Hall of Justice. The official city gallows stood nearby. Over a period of 20 years, 35 hangings were conducted here. Among those to die at the end of a rope was the notorious bandit Juan Flores.

The old Los Angeles Hall of Justice sits on the former site of hangings, gang shootouts, and a bordello.

By 1891, the gallows had been removed and a new courthouse stood at the site. Across East First Street, Morton's brothel ushered in a new era in which jurisprudence and sex replaced gunfights and hangings. In 1926, the current courthouse opened and soon became known as the legal stage for famous trials. In 1931, Clara "Tiger Woman" Phillips was incarcerated here after being convicted of killing her husband's mistress. In 1944, several zoot suiters were convicted of the Sleepy Lagoon murders. Their appeal exposed corruption in the DA's office and the convictions were later reversed. Robert Kennedy's killer, Sirhan Sirhan, was tried and convicted here, as was Charles Manson.

The city morgue once occupied the basement. Many victims of notorious murderers were autopsied here by famed coroner Dr. Thomas Noguchi. Also, the body of Marilyn Monroe was autopsied here, producing evidence that she committed suicide.

The courthouse was closed for many years for a major redesign and restoration, but ghost hunters find a lot of paranormal activity at several sites adjacent to the building. One investigator heard the exchange of shots, possibly a remnant of the *tong* wars that occurred here.

GHOST PROTESTOR AT CITY HALL

Los Angles City Hall
Temple and Main Streets
Los Angeles 90001
(213) 485-2121

Many citizens of Los Angeles exercise their right to protest government actions and political dealings at City Hall. They believe it is a civic responsibility to maintain a watchful eye over politicians and public officials. One citizen believed so strongly in his civic responsibility that he hasn't let death stop him. A man dressed in stylish clothing from the early 19th century has been seen interrupting city council meetings, trying to protest their proceedings. This ghost appears to recognize the environment and react to persons in the room. Therefore, this is a true ghostly appearance, not a haunting.

A noisy ghost protestor still roams Los Angeles City Hall seeking the attention of politicians.

The protestor has also appeared at various committee meetings, harassed city managers, and followed various officials through hallways. Visitors have seen him in the restrooms too. Cold spots have been identified just before the ghost makes an appearance.

Aside from his fine clothing, there are no clues as to the man's identity. The 28-story building, constructed in 1926, may occupy land owned by the ghost. One ghost hunter suspected that this ghost was a contractor who was not fully paid for his work on the building. Whatever his true identity, in life, his embarrassing political protests were so disruptive that henchmen silenced him.

Building staff and security guards have reported hauntings on floors 2, 3, 4, 27, and 28. The second floor is well known for apparitions and strange noises that come from several directions. On the 28th floor, closed-circuit TV cameras have displayed apparitions of several people floating about after the building is secured for the night.

FLOATING CANDLES

Mission San Gabriel
428 South Mission Drive
San Gabriel 91776
(626) 457-3035
www.sangabrielmission.org

San Gabriel was the fourth California mission founded by the Franciscan order headed by Father Junipero Serra. Located on a plain below the San Gabriel Mountains, this mission was the western terminus of the trail from Sonora, Mexico. Many who survived the long desert passage called it the "journey of death."

The first rough shelter to serve as a church was erected on September 8, 1771. In 1791, work began on the grand structure that still stands today. The church was dedicated in 1805 and stood as a beautiful centerpiece of the prosperous farms and ranches surrounding it. The unique bell tower collapsed in the earthquake of 1812, but it was rebuilt with stone. It stands with a row of huge buttresses that support four-foot-thick walls.

Several events occurred here that might explain the phantom candle that floats down the church aisle and into the courtyard. Various priests, craftsmen, teachers, and travelers died at the mission, together with hundreds of Indians. Famed mountain man Jedediah Smith and his men rested here in 1826. They were described as uncouth, filthy, and in poor health. Earlier, a Spanish soldier raped an Indian woman at the mission. When the woman's husband sought revenge, the soldier killed him. Following tradition, a candle was lit in the church for the dead man, who had been baptized a Catholic.

In the church, the candle floats about four feet off the floor, always moving from the altar toward the rear entrance. In the courtyard, the candle appears near the side door leading to the sanctuary.

Near the San Gabriel Mission, the ghost of an Indian man has been seen in homes and backyards. His apparition is visible for a few seconds, then he vanishes, leaving only a cold spot. A former reporter for the *Los Angeles Herald Examiner*, Wanda Sue Parrott, has collected hundreds of reports of this haunting from witnesses.

THE PHANTOM OF THE THEATRE

Variety Arts Center
940 Figueroa Street
Los Angeles 90001
(213) 362-0440

Dressed in a 16th-century costume, this ghost appears onstage at the Variety Arts Center without a cue or a clue. He bows with a graceful flourish to an unseen costar, then leaves the stage by disappearing rather than slipping into the wings. He seems oblivious to the set, scene, other actors, or stage crew.

Theatre manager Carl Fleming described this ghost to renowned paranormal investigator Dennis William Hauck as a male dressed as an Elizabethan, complete with plumed hat. No one has heard this phantom actor speak his lines, but he has impressed several people with his appearances. He shows up in rehearsals and well-attended performances. There is no historical information about the theatre or production companies that have worked here that might help identify this fellow.

THE LADY IN WHITE

La Golondrina Café
17 West Olvera Street
Los Angeles 90012
(213) 628-4349
http://www.lagolondrina.com/

An Italian, Guiseppi Covaccichi, built this brick house between 1855 and 1857, but lived here only a year. Between 1858 and 1871 four families lived here: the Garcias, Gazzos, Mascarels, and Reveras. Finally, in 1871, Antonio Pelanconi purchased the house. He lived here until his death in 1882, producing four children with his wife, Isabel Ramirez. An Italian became patriarch of the house once again when the widowed Isabel Pelanconi married Giaccomo Tononi. In

A ghostly lady in white wanders the second floor of La Golondrina Café on Olvera Street.

the 1950s, the two-story building known as the Pelanconi House became part of the El Pueblo de Los Angeles State Historic Park. Today, one of the best Mexican restaurants in Southern California occupies the first and second floors. The third floor is used for offices. Considering the large number of families who have lived in this house, and the possibility of a significant number of deaths, serious illnesses, and other deep, emotional events, it is no wonder that at least one ghost has been documented here. A young woman dressed in a flowing white gown has been seen in the restaurant and third-floor offices. Since seismic retrofitting was done in 1994-95, this ghost has been very active. This is an interesting phenomenon. When buildings are remodeled or replaced with newer structures, the spirits of earlier occupants seem to wake up and express their concern about the changes. During the retrofit, workers' tools were moved, doors were opened and closed, and electrical problems occurred. Several workers refused to work alone in the building.

Restaurant staff and patrons have reported cold spots and icy breezes at times when all windows and doors were closed. Disembodied footsteps have been heard on the third floor when no living soul was in the offices. Loud crashes, as if furniture has been overturned, have been heard as well.

Several people have seen the apparition of the lady in white drifting upstairs from the second to the third floor. The tendency of this ghost to favor the third floor suggests she was a member of the Pelanconi family. The children, Petra, Lorenzo, Honorina, and Isabel, used to sleep on this floor.

WIDOW'S GHOST

Avila Adobe
10 Olvera Street
Los Angeles 90012
(213) 628-1274
www.olvera-street.com

Former mayor of the Pueblo de Los Angeles, Francisco Avila built this house in 1818. Fully restored and open to the public, it is said to

The ghostly widow of Francisco Avila has been spotted at this historic Olvera Street home.

be the oldest house in Los Angeles. In his youth, Avila was known as a daredevil and a skilled horseman. He was quick to put on displays by riding through the streets, waving his lance, or swinging his lariat. He used these skills when he joined with others to oppose the harsh rule of the military governor, Lt. Col. Manuel Victoria. Marching south from the capital of Monterey, Victoria and his troops were met at Cahuega Pass by Avila and 150 insurgents. After a few shots were exchanged, many of the undisciplined insurgents fled. In an effort to rally his comrades, Avila leveled his lance and charged Victoria's second in command, Capt. Romualdo Pacheco. This brave act inspired the insurgents, turned the battle, and distracted Pacheco. As Avila continued his charge, he drew a pistol and shot Pacheco through the heart. As the fighting reached its peak, Avila was thrown from his horse and killed by the swords of loyal soldiers. Legend says that Lieutenant Colonel Victoria himself, nearly incapacitated by a lance wound in his face, inflicted the fatal wound.

Today, the house of Francisco Avila is a popular tourist attraction. Visitors who are fortunate enough to have quiet moments alone in the master bedroom have heard soft sobbing. One ghost hunter obtained recordings of this on tape. Psychic investigation of this location has detected a deep sense of sadness and loss. It is believed that this paranormal activity is a spirit remnant of Francisco Avila's wife mourning the loss of her valiant husband.

While visiting the Avila Adobe, ghost hunters might encounter paranormal activity at the Sepulveda House (1887), the large wooden cross at the south end of Olvera Street, the Historic Plaza (1825), the Old Plaza Church (1818), and the Pico House (1870) at 430 North Main Street.

THE LADY IN BLACK

Alexandria Hotel
501 South Spring Street
Los Angeles 90001
(213) 626-7484

When the Alexandria opened in 1906 it was in the heart of the

A ghost of a mysterious lady in black appears in the hallways of the Alexandria Hotel in downtown L.A.

theatre and movie communities in Southern California. This was the place silent-film stars, powerful producers, and talented directors met to conduct business and celebrate their successes. In 1919, the main dining room was used for a ceremony in which Charlie Chaplin, Mary Pickford, D. W. Griffith, and Douglas Fairbanks announced the formation of their independent movie company, United Artists. Big-band leader Paul Whiteman got his start in show biz by playing piano in the bar. The Alexandria's stately marble columns, stylish chandeliers, and fancy carpets inspired Charlie Chaplin to call it "the swankiest hotel in town."

In the 1970s the hotel underwent a complete overhaul and upgrade in order to maintain a competitive edge with newer hotels in Los Angeles and nearby Hollywood. Soon after it reopened, a mysterious woman appeared walking the halls. Hotel assistant manager, Nancy Malone, described the woman as almost solid, wearing a wide-brimmed hat with a veil and a beautiful black dress. The style of the dress, which had a gathering in the back described as a bustle, was late 19th century. This graceful ghost glides through the corridor without evoking a sense of threat or fear in those who see her. Instead, she gives the impression that she is in mourning and looking for someone or something in the hotel.

Ghost hunters Laurie Jacobsen and Marc Wanamaker suggest that this spirit may not have noticed her own death due to overwhelming grief she experienced in her later years. Now, she roams this romantic hotel, still grieving, searching for the loved one she lost.

Other ghost hunters have felt cold spots in the bar and lobby. Shadows and small, misty clouds have been seen on the stairs leading out of the lobby.

RAGS-TO-RICHES GHOST

Doheny Mansion
Doheny Campus of Mount Saint Mary's College
Chester Place
Los Angeles 90007-2518
(213) 477-2500

Ghost hunters and passersby often see strange shadows and soft lights in human shape in the windows of this magnificent mansion. These apparitions are too indistinct to identify the spirit responsible, but some believe the ghost of Edward L. Doheny haunts this historic home. Shadows, ethereal figures seen standing at the windows, cold spots in the downstairs hallway, and icy breezes indicate that at least one ghost haunts this mansion. Many believe the mournful face in the first-floor windows is that of Doheny's son, who died from a gunshot wound.

Edward Doheny personified the proverbial rags-to-riches legend. Son of an Irish laborer, he came to California in the late 1880s with wife and baby daughter in tow after an unsuccessful stint as a silver miner in Arizona. While living in a downtown, flea-infested Los Angeles hotel, he stood on the porch one day and watched a noisy wagon pass by hauling a load of foul-smelling, greasy black soil. Curious about this awful stuff, Doheny discovered that the oily substance could be used as fuel. With friend Charles Canfield, Doheny leased three acres and sunk a well. On April 20, 1893, he made history by opening the first free-flowing oil well in California. Within a few years, Doheny was one of the richest men in America.

Doheny's riches did not bring him endless happiness, however. For many years he had to fight federal charges of bribery and conspiracy. These lengthy legal battles damaged his health and dulled his spirit. His frail daughter died at age seven, and his only son was shot by a friend who then committed suicide.

Edward Doheny died in his mansion at age 79 in 1935. His wife, Estelle, followed him in 1958. Their generosity guaranteed that the Doheny name would be forever known in Southern California. Libraries at the University of Southern California and St. John's Seminary in Camarillo, the Estelle Doheny Eye Foundation, two historic mansions, a landmark beach, and several public edifices built with Doheny money are the most prominent signs of the family's legacy.

Having spent most of his wealthy years fighting charges of criminal business practices and bribery of federal officials, Edward Doheny was never free to put the hardships of his life behind him and enjoy his good fortune. Perhaps now, many years after his death, he roams his Chester Place mansion, finally able to relax in its luxuries, released from the miseries that filled the life of a very rich man.

GHOST BANKER AT THE BALZAC CAFÉ

722 North Azusa Boulevard
Azusa 91702
(626) 334-4343

This charming café serves savory Middle Eastern food and houses some lively early-20th-century ghosts. The Balzac Café occupies a historic brick building that for many years was a bank. Thick walls and a massive concrete foundation no doubt account for its longevity. Ghosts seem to like the sturdy building too. Restaurant staff report odd noises coming from unoccupied areas, cold spots, unexplained icy breezes, and shadows. The pale apparition of a tall gentleman dressed in an elegant tuxedo also appears here. He seems to be an older man with a beard. This ghost, known as the banker, roams through the second-floor offices making sure the business end of the restaurant is run properly. On occasion, he makes an appearance downstairs, surprising some of the patrons by looking over the food they've ordered. Many believe this is a spirit remnant of a former bank official or owner.

The apparition of a young woman is also seen at the Balzac Café. She appears in the dining room and in the area near the women's restroom. This ghost seems to be confused by the busy restaurant and the people dining in the old bank.

People connected with the Balzac Café are unable to identify these ghosts. Local historians do not know of any events that might have created these hauntings or might have bound these spirits to the old bank.

GHOST PILOTS

200 Block of North Soldano Avenue
Azusa 91702

There is something strange about North Soldano Avenue in the eastside town of Azusa. Walking along this street, particularly on the 200 block, you get a creepy feeling that something tragic happened here. As you pass by the vacant lot, the feeling gets stronger and it's joined by the notion that someone is there, but you can't see him or her. Ghost hunters who have walked through this vacant lot report hearing disembodied cries for help. Some have seen the pale apparitions of two women with terrified, painful expressions reaching out, trying to catch someone's attention.

Few people in the neighborhood are willing to talk about this place, but some say this patch of ground is haunted. Ghost hunters Robert and Anne Wlodarski uncovered some information about a plane crash at this location. A limited search of newspaper archives and Federal Aviation Administration records of aviation accidents did not turn up any airplane crashes that might have occurred here since 1985. One longtime resident reported that the crash occurred in the early '70s.

The story goes that a small plane carrying two women pilots crashed on North Soldano Avenue, destroying a small house that had stood here since the early '50s. The pilots were either trapped in the wreckage or so injured that they could not extricate themselves. The ensuing fire burned the women to death. Since then, their ghosts have roamed the site, crying out for help. Their haunting has created such a tragic atmosphere that no one has built a house on the property.

Some believe these ghosts wander the neighborhood. In fact, a few blocks away, at the corner of Foothill Boulevard and North Soldano Avenue, stands a 1920s-vintage house—a former playhouse—that is reported to be home to several ghosts. Some of these ghosts have been seen in the adjacent Azusa City Park.

GHOST BOYS

John Anson Ford Park
800 Park Lane
Cudahy 90201
(562) 806-7662

People who have lived near this park for many years can point out the location of a grisly double murder that occurred here in late 1972. A search of *Los Angeles Times* archives could not corroborate their stories, but ghost hunters have encountered spirit remnants of the two victims. Their descriptions of the ghosts' characteristics match details recalled by locals who witnessed the police investigation and cleanup of the murder scene.

On a warm late-October evening, two boys entered the park to fish in the pond. In the morning, their bodies were found in a pool of blood. The assailants had cut the boys' throats with large knives and disappeared without a trace. Local police suspect this was a gang-initiation murder. More than 30 years later, the ghosts of the boys still hang out at the park. The ghost most often sighted is described as short with spiky hair and blue eyes. Ghost hunters report that he does not appear angry or frightened, but he vanishes if you approach him too fast or get too close. The other boy appears as fog that glows with a soft white light. Some visitors to this location report the sound of footsteps, as if someone is running on the grass, and disembodied voices. Balls of light, known as "orbs" by ghost hunters, have also been reported.

JERRY LYNN'S GHOST

Aztec Hotel
311 West Foothill Boulevard
Monrovia 91016
(626) 358-3231

Built in 1924, this structure, inspired by Aztec and Mayan architecture, opened as a respectable hotel but soon declined. The guest rooms were then used as a bordello, and a speakeasy opened in the basement. It seems that the hotel was revamped in the 1930s and became a fashionable stopover for many stars, including Fred Astaire, Errol Flynn, Ava Gardner, Ginger Rogers, Frank Sinatra, Katherine Hepburn, and Spencer Tracy.

In 1929 a woman named Jerry Lynn lived in room 129. It is not known if she was a prostitute, member of the hotel staff, or legitimate resident. A longtime employee described Jerry as tall, thin, beautiful, and about 25 years old. She had quite a romance with a famous actor, but he ended the affair to avoid damage to his career. Jerry was so upset that she committed suicide in her room one night while two floors below, the speakeasy patrons toasted the end of Prohibition. Since that night in 1929, Jerry's ghost has been trapped in the building. Her apparition has been seen walking the corridor outside her room, dressed in a tasteful tan dress with matching gloves and high-heeled shoes. She also wears a wide-brim hat that was quite fashionable for the time. This elegant ghost has been seen near the stairs on the second floor and in the downstairs women's restroom. Hotel guests have experienced freezing temperatures in this room even on very hot days when the building's air conditioner has failed. Several problems with heating and alarm systems have also been attributed to Jerry's ghost.

Based on witness accounts, ghost hunters believe this spirit remnant is not angry or vengeful, but merely stuck at this location. Psychic investigation may reveal her reasons for continuing her stay at the Aztec Hotel.

AGITATED ENTITIES

El Pollo Loco
123 East Holt Avenue
Pomona 91768
(909) 622-2275

This restaurant used to be known as the Charles Grill. Ghost hunters Robert and Anne Wlodarski reported a vast array of paranormal activity indicating that several spirit entities reside here. Restaurant staff and customers have heard anxious voices and loud arguments coming from areas of the building that are unoccupied. This auditory phenomena is brief, somewhat muffled, and occurs as such a surprise that witnesses don't clearly hear what is said.

Disembodied footsteps and slamming doors often follow the ghostly arguments. Some customers report the appearance of tense, strange-looking people standing in the corridors leading to the restrooms and in other parts of the restaurant. When restaurant managers investigate, only happy people are found enjoying good food and pleasant atmosphere.

The Wlodarskis also reported potted plants bent so that their tops touch the floor. They stay in this position for minutes, then spring back.

Little is known of the building's history that might help identify the spirit entities and their reasons for occupying the site. The tri-level building is unusual and at one time might have been an apartment building, offices, or a boarding house where people unfamiliar with each other might have had conflicts that led to arguments.

It is interesting that the Charles Grill went out of business at this location. A rapid turnover of businesses often indicates something more than poor management and bad luck. Frequently, a particular building might sit on a Native American burial site, a former cemetery, or an unmarked death site.

GHOST CHILDREN OF DOMINGUEZ RANCHO

Dominguez Rancho Adobe
18127 Alameda Street
Rancho Dominguez 90220
(310) 603-0088

This historic adobe was the hub of a giant rancho established as Rancho San Pedro by Don Juan Jose Dominguez in 1784. It was made possible by a grant of 75,000 acres received from King Carlos III of Spain as a gift for loyal military service. The land was so vast that today it encompasses the cities of Compton, Gardena, Carson, Torrance, San Pedro, Harbor City, Wilmington, all the Palos Verdes Peninsula, and parts of Long Beach.

In 1826, Manuel Dominguez, the nephew of Don Juan, built a large adobe house for his new bride, Maria Engracia. Maria gave birth to ten children in this house. Unfortunately, four of them died here while very young. Manuel also died in this house in 1882, leaving his six daughters to divide the rancho, giving them sizable dowries.

Situated on the southern approach to the Los Angeles Basin, the rancho was the site of skirmishes between Indians and Mexican soldiers in the 1830s. During the brief Mexican-American War of 1846,

The historic Dominguez Adobe was the hub of a 75,000-acre rancho.

U.S. Marines disembarked in San Pedro and chased Mexican soldiers across the rolling hills to the Pueblo of Los Angeles. After the war, bandits sometimes roamed the hills preying on stagecoaches or unwary travelers. One such episode is described in a later story, "Dead Southerner."

In the Dominguez adobe, ghost hunters have encountered orbs and streaks of light together with cold spots. Some investigators believe these are spirit remnants of the Dominguez children who died in this house. Quiet meditation in the Victorian Carson room, named for one of the six daughters, can result in a palpable sense of the 1840s, complete with odors of dust from the fields, food, and animal skins. One ghost hunter detected a thickened atmosphere to the right of the fireplace that seemed masculine. Perhaps this is the patriarch, Don Juan, or his nephew Don Manuel Dominguez.

ROSE GARDEN GHOSTS

Exposition Park Rose Garden
Exposition Boulevard between Figueroa and Menlo Avenues
Los Angeles 90007

This fantastic rose garden adorns acreage adjacent to the famous Los Angeles Coliseum, across the street from the University of Southern California. Opened in 1876 as a show ground for agricultural and horticultural products, the area soon deteriorated and became overrun with gangs, bums, and thieves. By 1890, the place stood in stark contrast to the young, flourishing university community across the street. Appalled by the crime and slovenly appearance of the old agricultural park, civic leaders placed the land in the hands of Los Angeles County. The county built three large buildings to house a museum, a National Guard armory, and an exposition hall.

In 1928, the rose garden was completed with paths, fountains, and sitting areas. The European-style garden, composed of nearly 16,000 rosebushes, attracted the high society of Los Angeles and served as a beautiful concourse for the 1932 Olympic Games staged at the Coliseum.

From its very beginning, the rose garden was a place for L.A. society to take strolls and attend exclusive parties. Some of these parties were important civic functions at the museum affording an opportunity for up-and-comers to be seen with the established rich and famous. For many people, these special events were the highlight of their lives. So much so that some of these folks are still here, enjoying the promenades among the roses.

Hauntings comprised of partial apparitions of men and women dressed in clothing of the 1920s and '30s have been seen here. A stylish couple takes a turn around the central fountain, walking about ten to 15 feet before disappearing. Reports say this apparition appears several times within a few minutes just before sunset. Nearby, the partial apparition of a tall black hat and cape have appeared, floated a few feet, then vanished. The image of a girl dressed in white lace appears in the first row of roses at the west side of the central fountain.

NOISY GHOSTS OF THE BIG BOX STORE

Fontana Big Lots Store
17575 Foothill Boulevard
Fontana 9235
(909) 355-0763

Several ghosts haunt this huge building. Descriptions of paranormal activity also suggest poltergeist events occur here. However, parapsychologists believe the living may create these strange phenomena.

In both restrooms occupants of toilet stalls hear the sound of objects falling from the ceiling to the floor. Yet, when the occupant emerges from the stall, no one else is in the room, and nothing is found on the floor. Lights in these rooms also turn off and on. Invisible hands pull paper towels from the dispenser.

In some of the employees-only areas, disembodied voices are heard, lights are turned on and off, and doors are slammed. In an area designated "warehouse," voices have been heard in an argument. One employee entered this area to dispose of trash. As she was leaving, the lights went out and a hand pulled her hair out of its tightly coiled bun. She was found pale and shaken. When she regained her composure, she quit her job at the store.

A ghost hunter who walked the aisles at midday noticed a shadowy presence, thickened atmosphere, and cold spots. Many of the newer big-box stores are haunted. The Toys "R" Us in Sunnyvale, California, is haunted by a man who died at the site a century before the building was constructed. Psychic Sylvia Browne, who contacted that ghost, believes hauntings such as this occur because spirit remnants are confused by changes in the site. These ghosts may be trying to get the attention of living souls in order to find out what happened to the farm or ranch that was their home.

The possibility of poltergeist activity at this site remains to be investigated.

Also on Foothill Boulevard, between cross streets Citrus and Cherry Avenues, the ghost of a young man appears. Dressed in a striped shirt and dark pants, he carries a long stick or buggy whip. This ghost crosses the street mid-block, causing drivers to hit the brakes. An instant before impact, the man vanishes. This ghost has also been reported walking alongside the road escorted by a black dog on a leash.

SPIRITS OF THE MASSACRE

Rio Hondo Riverbed
Veterans Park (Zindell Avenue) and South Bluff Road at Slauson Avenue
Pico Rivera 90660

From the time Spanish explorers first arrived in Southern California to the beginning of the Mexican period in 1820, countless conflicts occurred between the soldiers who guarded the mission and Indians. Mission records reveal many incidents in which soldiers abused, molested, even raped Indian women. When Indian men rose up in their defense, they were sometimes killed. Often the offending soldiers were sent back to Mexico only to be replaced by others who thought the Indians were inferior beings not protected by the Spanish crown or the Catholic Church.

In September 1998, construction workers at the ARCO refinery in Carson uncovered the remains of more than 50 Gabrielino Indians. The remains of those 200-year-old Indians indicated the individuals had died from violent trauma. Many had broken bones. One man's spinal column was snapped backward, placing his head near his pelvis. Some of the women died with their hands crossed over their faces. Although no one has found evidence of their involvement, it is believed that Spanish soldiers committed this atrocity. Archaeological evidence found elsewhere suggests that tragedies such as this might have occurred much more often than history books suggest.

The haunting of the Rio Hondo riverbed in Pico Rivera may be evidence that such a conflict occurred at that site. Visitors to the area, and some ghost hunters, have heard the sound of musket fire—not that of modern firearms—and screaming coming from the riverbed. The sound tends to move from north to south, suggesting victims of the massacre were chased by their attackers. Most screams are female voices and the musket fire is sporadic. One ghost hunter heard the pounding of horse hoofs on sand or gravel. The town of Pico Rivera was not founded until the 1870s, and its recorded history does not list conflicts between farmers, ranchers, or the railroads as a possible basis of this haunting.

There are two vantage points for this haunting. The most accessible is Veterans Park at the foot of Zindell Avenue. The other is South Bluff Road off Slauson Avenue. The nearby freeway requires that ghost hunters use a technique such as meditation to block out modern sounds.

DEAD SOUTHERNER

Del Amo Boulevard, between South Wilmington Avenue and South Alameda Street
Carson 90810

In 1865, this region comprised the Dominguez Rancho. One of its ranch houses was used as a stagecoach stop for lines connecting the port of San Pedro with the Pueblo of Los Angeles. The crossroads were busy, but passengers who stopped here for rest and a meal found themselves scrutinized by local cowboys, farmers, petty thieves, and businessmen. All staunch Union supporters during the Civil War, when their patriotic fervor was aroused, these rough people could be belligerent and dangerous.

One day in June 1865, a passenger disembarked from a stage and struck up a conversation with one of the locals. His Southern accent was obvious and as the conversation continued, he revealed his political affiliations. In moments, a crowd gathered and tempers flared. The Southerner must have assumed that the law would protect him and he continued criticizing Abraham Lincoln and the Yankee Congress.

Someone in the crowd drew a pistol and struck the man with its butt. At that point, the crowd became a mob of thieves. They dragged the unwary fellow behind a shed, beat him, robbed him of his money, hat, and boots, then hauled him to a nearby tree and hung him.

That horrible death left an imprint on the area. In spite of the heavy traffic on these main thoroughfares, people often see a man dressed in 1860s clothing standing near the corner of Del Amo Boulevard and South Wilmington Avenue. He appears confused, as if he does not know which way to go to escape the angry mob that pursues him. This poor fellow has also been seen walking west along Del Amo Boulevard, near the intersection with South Alameda Street.

GHOST MOM

Agua Mansa Pioneer Cemetery
2001 West Agua Mansa Road
Colton 92324-3388
(909) 370-2091

The ghost of a woman has been seen floating through this old cemetery. She appears pale, nearly transparent, but details of her face, hair, and upper body are easily discernible. Typical of human apparitions, her feet and lower legs are not visible. She is Hispanic, young, with long hair, and she moves about paying no attention to the living souls visiting the graveyard. Ghost hunters who have witnessed this apparition conclude that she is looking for her children. She may be buried some distance from the graves of her children and she now wanders about in search of them.

The Agua Mansa Pioneer Cemetery was established in the 1840s soon after the twin villages of La Placita and Agua Mansa were founded on opposite banks of the Santa Ana River. Thriving farms and ranches fostered rapid growth of the populations of these communities. In the 1840s, however, people died at an age now considered young. Injuries, infections, communicable diseases, and childbirth all contributed to the growing population of the cemetery.

In 1862, the Santa Ana River overflowed its banks, nearly destroying the nearby village of Agua Mansa. Only the cemetery, chapel, and Cornelius Jensen's store remained after the water receded. There are no records of deaths caused by the flood but one headstone records the death of a young woman who died in 1862.

The young woman who haunts this peaceful cemetery may have lost her life in the flood of 1862 only to return in search of her children.

They may be buried in graves that are unmarked or marked with headstones that are no longer readable. It is also possible that the children were carried away by the flood and died in the muddy water at an unknown location miles downstream.

CHAPTER 4

South Los Angeles, Long Beach, and Orange County

THE MOST HAUNTED SHIP IN AMERICA

The *Queen Mary*
1126 Queen's Highway
Long Beach 90802-6390
(562) 435-3511
www.queenmary.com

It has been said that every ship is haunted, especially older vessels. The presence of ghosts is always part of the legend of great ships, creating a bit of mystery that fires the imagination and makes us want to go to sea. The majestic *Queen Mary* has plenty of legends, mysteries, and, by last count, at least 600 ghosts. Permanently docked in Long Beach, this magnificent ocean liner is much more than a fascinating museum. The *Queen Mary* is a major Southern California tourist attraction that includes a 365-room hotel, wedding chapel, and several restaurants and bars.

This massive ship was launched on the Clyde River, Scotland, on September 26, 1934, and christened by King George V. It was not until May 27, 1936, that she embarked on her maiden voyage with 1,742 passengers and 1,186 crew. In the course of her sailing career, the *Queen Mary* made 1,001 Atlantic crossings. She carried two million passengers, including 800,000 American troops during World War II.

During her 31 years at sea, several people died onboard. The official total is 55, including 37 passengers, 16 crew, and two GIs. The unofficial total exceeds 600.

The Queen Mary *in Long Beach is believed to be the most haunted ship in America.*

On October 2, 1942, the *Queen Mary* collided with the escort ship HMS *Curacao* off the coast of Ireland in broad daylight. The smaller *Curacao* crossed the bow of the *Queen* and was sliced in half. Three hundred thirty-eight of the *Curacao's* crew were killed in the incident. Ghost hunters and psychics believe hundreds of them occupy the lower decks of the *Queen Mary* near the bow of the ship. Their moans and sobs have been heard as an echo in the dark passageways.

During World War II, the *Queen Mary* carried hundreds if not thousands of prisoners of war from North Africa to England and the U.S. Psychic investigations revealed that many POWs died aboard the ship. They were stuffed into canvas bags and buried at sea without documentation. Psychic Debbie Christensen Senate conducted a spirit communication session in which she channeled an Italian pilot named Carlo who described this kind of treatment. Carlo and other POWs are still imprisoned on the lower decks. Both visitors and the ship's security staff have reported moans, cries, sobs, and voices speaking in Italian.

The list of haunted rooms and compartments is quite long and includes the sun deck, officers' quarters, several passageways, and many staterooms that are now part of the hotel. Paranormal activity has been reported in rooms A-110, A-136, A-170, B-123, B-340, B-409, M-127, M-147, and M-220. Room B-340 is fascinating. When the ship was underway, this was a third-class cabin. A jealous husband murdered a purser here. The young man's ghost haunts this room, creating so many disturbances that it is no longer offered for guest accommodations.

On July 10, 1966, during a routine test of the automated watertight doors, crewman John Pedder realized he was not at his duty station. Fearing the wrath of his chief, the 18-year-old sailor raced along the narrow passageway, past one of the propeller drive shafts, headed for door number 13. As he approached the door there appeared to be just enough space to slide under it before it slammed shut. Door number 13 turned out to be unlucky for John Pedder. He was crushed to death. Years later, he is still trying to slide under that door. The apparition of this unlucky sailor is one of the most often sighted on the *Queen Mary*. He is known as "the Shaft Alley Specter."

Senior Second Officer W. E. Stark is also sighted frequently in his quarters and on the forward decks. Stark died September 22, 1949. A few days earlier, at the end of his shift, he sat down to enjoy a glass of gin. He didn't know that someone had replaced the gin with carbon tetrachloride and lime juice, and failed to place a poison label on the bottle. It is thought that Stark is still searching for evidence that points to his murderer.

Apparitions of several other crew members have been sighted in the kitchen, engine rooms, boiler rooms, engineering spaces, and the passageways connecting these areas. At times, entire crews are seen tending the boilers or engines, shouting orders, or calling for assistance. Psychic investigations have detected a switchboard operator, purser, butler, and matron in charge of stewardesses.

The Lady in White is one of the best known ghosts aboard the *Queen Mary*. Her gown is shimmering white and backless, the height of fashion in the late 1930s. She appears in the main dining room walking with an elegant gait, nodding to unseen guests. Then she moves on to the first-class lounge, where she lingers, listening to the piano. Some witnesses have seen her dance alone, turning gracefully across the floor before vanishing.

In the main ballroom, the apparitions of more than 20 people have been seen enjoying a grand party. Dressed in elegant evening attire, they dance, drink, sing, and laugh the night away. Their banter is accented with the sounds of popping Champagne corks.

Other hot spots for ghost hunters include the first-class swimming pool, Promenade Café, first-class nursery exhibit, and bridge. At several locations throughout the ship, people appear dressed in clothing of the 1930s and '40s. They may be ghosts or the staff of the Queen Mary Hotel.

THE GHOST GUNNERS OF FORT MACARTHUR

Fort MacArthur Museum
3601 South Gaffey Street
San Pedro 90731
(310) 548-2631
www.ftmac.org

The long, narrow corridors formed by massive concrete walls seal the fort from sunlight, fresh breezes, and the passage of time. Cool, still air and muted shadows make visitors feel as though they've traveled back in time to World War II, when Fort MacArthur guarded the Los Angeles harbor against attack by Japanese naval forces. Standing in the rear gallery, the shell room, or the truck corridor, ghost hunters have heard the sound of combat boots step across the concrete floor. They have not only felt sudden icy breezes, but ghost hunters have even heard the muted rattle of machinery that hasn't been used in 50 years.

Fort MacArthur was established in 1914 on land that was used in the early 1800s as a landing place by the Spanish army. Between 1810 and 1846, various military facilities were constructed here as the harbor grew and California changed from Spanish to Mexican, then American hands. On the eve of World War I, construction of a sprawling, heavily fortified facility was begun and named in honor of Lt. Gen. Arthur MacArthur, father of Douglas MacArthur. Huge guns were placed here that could fire a 1,400-pound projectile 27 miles. Additional gun emplacements, called batteries, were installed in the 1930s. After World War II, the fort's massive guns were considered obsolete and replaced with 18 Nike missile launch sites. Then, in 1977, the army declared the fort as surplus property and deeded most of the land to the City of Los Angeles. Today, gun batteries Osgood and Farley, their interconnecting passageways and compartments, are known as the Fort MacArthur Museum.

During the years of the Second World War, thousands of military personnel served here, inspired by the courage of overseas troops and determined to ward off any attack on the L.A. harbor region. An attack, such as the one that devastated Pearl Harbor, was not only considered a possibility, but at times, eminent. Anxious days of training, drilling, and waiting for an attack left a mark on this place. The ghosts of shell runners, powder monkeys, and gunnery sergeants may still be on duty here, waiting for the order to fire their guns.

MURDER VICTIM OF THE VILLA DEL SOL

Brownstone Café
305 North Harbor Boulevard #115
Fullerton 92832
(714) 526-9123

For many years, this location at the heart of Fullerton was an odiferous feedlot. By 1917, a lumberyard that was less offensive, but still not an attractive feature of this growing community had replaced the livestock and manure piles. Recognizing the value of the land and location, 200 citizens joined Charles C. Chapman and invested $250,000 in the construction of the magnificent California Hotel. This Spanish Colonial Revival building, constructed in a U shape to create a large courtyard, housed luxury apartments, 55 hotel rooms, and several shops and restaurants. On opening day, January 15, 1923, the California Hotel became the jewel of downtown Fullerton. Ultimately, the ravage of years, including some unsavory activities

The ghost of a 1930s murder victim is believed to haunt the Brownstone Café in the historic Villa del Sol of Fullerton.

during Prohibition, caused the hotel to lose its luster. On the eve of the hotel's demolition in 1964, plans for renovation were unveiled and the building was saved. The building was converted into offices, shops, and a restaurant. The California Hotel reopened in 1965 as the Villa del Sol.

As with several other sites described in this book, renovation or demolition and new construction often arouses the interests of spirits who reside in a building or at a location. In 2000, a paranormal investigation conducted by the Orange County Society for Psychic Research, led by Michael Kouri, stated that the entire building is psychically charged with emotional imprints and is occupied by several spirits. This investigation revealed that numerous tragic events occurred here, including unnatural deaths, many of which were suicides.

The ghost who visits the Brownstone Café is believed to be a spirit remnant of a 1930s murder victim. The crime could be associated with a speakeasy (a bar that served illegal liquor) that occupied part of the California Hotel. This fellow was discovered after an alarm system, including motion detectors, was installed. The detectors were activated in sequence as if someone were walking through the kitchen after the restaurant had closed. One night, the manager was present when the alarms were tripped. He felt a presence, as if someone were standing next to him. When he turned to dash out the door, he was hit by a blast of cold air. A moment later, a heavy metal pot hit the floor with a loud crash.

Throughout the restaurant, both staff and patrons have detected cold spots, disembodied footsteps, moving objects, knocking sounds, and a feeling that some invisible being is standing nearby or looking over their shoulder. Humming is also heard, especially when 1930s-era music is played. The sound of two disembodied voices has been heard inside the entrance. These ghosts are quiet, sometimes mumbling.

Aside from the kitchen ghost, ghosts hunters believe several other spirits frequent the Brownstone Café, including two adult female spirits, one little girl, an angry man, and a curious old man who likes to read the menu.

ROAMING SPIRITS OF THE VILLA DEL SOL

Café Hidalgo
305 North Harbor Boulevard #111
Fullerton 92832
(714) 447-3203

Some of the spirits who wander through the Brownstone Café, described above, also make appearances in Café Hidalgo. Ghost hunters Robert and Anne Wlodarski suggest modern renovations of the Villa del Sol may have eliminated large rooms, hallways, or other places to which spirits are attached. As a result, a ghost may appear to pass through walls, from one business or apartment to another, as if he is strolling a hallway where he died or exiting a room in which he was murdered. The murder victim believed to haunt the Brownstone Café also manifests at Café Hidalgo. Objects move, strange noises are heard, cold spots appear, and icy breezes hit people who are far from doors or windows.

One report says a ghost threw a tape across a room, where it landed next to the stereo. Apparently, this spirit was trying to get two employees to play the tape. His selection was Credence Clearwater.

One of the ghosts who passes through this café knows the name of the manager. He whispered the name, unnerving the fellow.

GHOST STORIES AT THE STADIUM TAVERN

305 North Harbor Boulevard
Fullerton 92832
(714) 447-4200

This great sports bar and restaurant is part of the haunted Villa del Sol described above. Ghosts who wander through Café Hidalgo and the Brownstone Café sometimes show up here, creating cold spots, moving objects, mumbling, or whispering to patrons and staff. One of these ghosts, a fellow named Chuck, was a frequent customer of Heroes Restaurant. When that business moved a few blocks away, Chuck remained on his favorite barstool in the new Stadium Tavern.

Manager Tom Dow hasn't seen Chuck, but employees in neighboring businesses know he is around. One woman, who declined to be

The Stadium Tavern in Fullerton was an illegal bar in the Prohibition era of the 1920s. Ghostly spirits still hang out with live visitors who come to hear the manager tell ghost stories. (Photo by T. W. Storer.)

named, has seen Chuck enter the Stadium Tavern early in the morning. Others believe Chuck creates a cold spot over his cherished place at the bar to ward off living customers.

On Halloween and other occasions, Tom Dow takes regular customers, and a few ghost hunters, downstairs to his offices for a special treat. After turning off the lights, Tom reads stories about the ghosts of the Villa del Sol, inviting spirits to join the party. This area is believed to be the site of offices and backrooms for the speakeasy that operated here in the 1920s. Historians and ghost hunters suspect that at least one murder was committed here.

DISQUIETED SPIRITS

Fullerton Police Station
237 West Commonwealth Avenue
Fullerton 92832
(714) 738-6800
www.cityoffullerton.com/depts/police/

When the Fullerton Police Station was constructed in 1941, human bones were unearthed and tossed aside. At that time, construction crews were not aware of their importance and state laws protecting such discoveries did not exist. Later, when a state archeologist was brought in to determine the age, ethnicity, and possible cause of death of the long-dead individuals, it became clear that an important burial ground was not only desecrated but also destroyed. So, it isn't any wonder that the building erected over the site is haunted.

Visitors to the police station, office staff, and law enforcement personnel have reported the partial apparition of a man moving through the corridors of the building. Of course, police officers are reluctant to report their experiences, but others talk of this chilling figure that appears disturbed or angry. He has long, dark hair that appears matted and tied with string or a strip of leather. Only his upper body is seen, sometimes with only one arm.

Disembodied footsteps are also heard moving through the hallways, together with indistinct sounds described as tapping, grunting, humming, and muffled chanting.

TUNNEL GHOSTS OF FULLERTON

Plummer Auditorium
201 East Chapman Avenue
Fullerton 92832-1925
(717) 870-2913

There is something bizarre about Fullerton. This nice, typical Southern California city has a secret that only a few people will talk about, but if you can get a longtime resident to join you in a quiet café for coffee, you may be let in on it.

Persistent ghost hunters have learned that a network of tunnels runs under the heart of the city. The tunnels were constructed in stages and for various purposes. Pioneers, bootleggers, criminals, and many others with something to hide or a destination that had be reached without witnesses contributed to these tunnels. One of the entrances lies under the Plummer Auditorium, built in 1930. It seems the tunnels are full of ghosts or spirit remnants from the days when bodies were disposed of down there. Criminals succumbed to wounds, kidnap victims died of exposure, or unlucky adventurers became lost in the tunnels of Fullerton.

Locals will tell you that the maze of tunnels is accessible from Plummer Auditorium—and other spots in town—but no one will divulge the location of its concealed doors because there is some scary stuff down there. Ghost hunters report a man dressed in World War II-era clothing who appears in the auditorium then disappears through an unseen trap door in the floor. There are reports of visitors being pushed by invisible hands as they walk the auditorium aisles. Some visitors have been slammed against the walls. Chandeliers sometimes sway then stop abruptly, defying gravity, then continue to swing.

Others claim to have walked through the tunnels and encountered several ghosts from various periods of the region's history. In a long, straight tunnel directly under Plummer Auditorium, the man in World War II attire appears and escorts ghost hunters to the exit before vanishing.

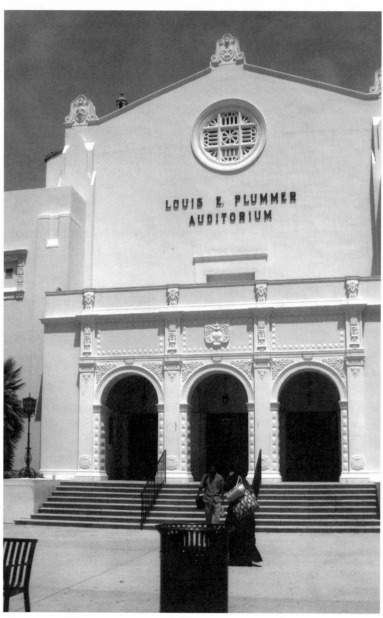

Plummer Auditorium in Fullerton may be a portal for ghosts who wander the tunnel under the city.

GHOST PHILOSOPHER

Stanley Ranch Museum
12174 Euclid Avenue
Garden Grove 92840
(714) 530-8871

The gingerbread-style 1891 Ware-Stanley House is the central feature of the two-acre Heritage Park Museum. Several buildings have been moved to the site from nearby locations to preserve the architectural history of Garden Grove. Among the more interesting structures are the fire station, tank house, and the blacksmith shop. These buildings are good targets for psychic investigation and ghost hunts. The Stanley House is already a documented haunted site with at least three ghosts.

This quaint two-story house was built in 1891-92 by horticulturist Edward G. Ware. His daughter, Lillian Agnes, married Arthur C. Stanley and moved into the house after the death of her parents. A caretaker, Don H., who lived in the house in the 1970s, experienced numerous encounters with a ghost who offered an interesting philosophy. One night, while Don rested on his bed, an older man appeared dressed in farmer's clothing. The ghost advised Don, "Don't take any bullshit," then disappeared. Each time the ghost appeared, he gave some sage advice.

Visitors to the house have sensed the presence of the ghost philosopher—probably Edward G. Ware—and other spirits. Some have heard the sound of a baby crying in the upstairs nursery. Others have detected an adult female presence just outside that room. This may be the ghost of Mrs. Ware rushing to attend her sick baby. Psychic investigation indicates a baby did indeed die in the crib, but historical research indicates it was the child of a caretaker. Also, on the stairs, psychics get the impression of pain and frustration. The emotions are so strong it makes sensitive people feel as though they might not make it to the landing. This has been interpreted as an imprint from Agnes Stanley who in her final years was unable to climb the stairs and visit the room she occupied as a child. Agnes's ghost is believed to approach the stairs, then turn away, saddened by her confinement to the first floor.

Nearby, Arthur Stanley's 1922 barn ages in the shade of a huge tree. Today, it is used to store books and other donated items sold to raise funds for the museum, but the barn was once used as a playhouse.

The 1890 Stanley House in Garden Grove is home to the ghosts of Agnes Stanley and Edward G. Ware.

During rehearsals for various plays, an older, well-dressed man was often seen sitting in the front row, captivated by the actors on stage. He was seen by several people and appeared so lifelike that he was often presumed to be a relative of one of the performers. When approached, however, he would disappear. Some have alleged that photographs taken during performances show unusual lights shaped like lightning bolts. Ghost hunters have interpreted these lights as spirit energy.

THE PINK LADY OF THE YORBA FAMILY CEMETERY

Old Yorba Linda Cemetery
6749 Parkwood Court
Yorba Linda 92886
(714) 528-4260

In 1858 Don Bernardo Yorba set aside this small piece of land as a final resting place for members of his large family. His imposing head-stone is surrounded by no less than 30 graves containing the remains of the Yorbas and their relatives by marriage. Over the years, other Southern California pioneers and historical figures were buried here with the consent of Yorba family leaders. Names such as Carrillo, Peralta, Dominguez, Sepulveda, and Castillo can be found on many grave markers. Don Bernardo's daughter, Alvina de Los Reyes, is buried here too. But unlike most who occupy this ground, she is not at rest.

Late at night on June 15, 1898, while returning from a fiesta, Alvina's carriage overturned, killing her. Later, in even-numbered years, she began making appearances on the anniversary of her death. Her apparition glows with a pink light, giving her the title the "Pink Lady." Ghost hunters report that Alvina wanders the graveyard, paus-ing to weep over an unmarked grave. The anniversary of Alvina's death is a big event in Yorba Linda. Many people gather at the ceme-tery on June 15, hoping to spot the pink ghost who has haunted this place for more than a century.

There are other spirits around, though, that appear more often. Many believe the ghost of Josefa Carrillo walks this graveyard too. Senorita Josefa was the heir of one of the richest founding families of old California. Upon reaching the age to marry, Josefa was pursued by an American sea captain, Henry Delano Fitch, and Lt. Col. Jose Echeandia, governor of California. On the day she married Fitch, Echeandia sat in his San Diego office seething with anger that a for-eigner should win such a prize. In spite of the long and happy life they shared, Captain Fitch was buried elsewhere. Now, Josefa walks the cemetery searching for her husband's grave.

AN EVIL PRESENCE

Rancho Los Cerritos Adobe
4600 Virginia Road
Long Beach 90807
(562) 570-1755
www.rancholoscerritos.org

The ranch was established in 1784 on a 300,000-acre land grant

The ghost of a former ranch foreman has been detected at Rancho Los Cerritos by professional ghost hunters and psychics.

given by the king of Spain to Manuel Nieto as reward for his military service in the exploration of California. By 1790, boundary disputes with Mission San Gabriel reduced the size of Nieto's holdings to 167,000 acres. In 1834, Nieto's daughter, Manuela Cota, received 27,000 acres known as El Rancho de Los Cerritos (Ranch of the Little Hills). She and her husband, Guillermo, raised 12 children in their adobe home and developed a successful cattle business. After her death in December 1843, her heirs sold the ranch to John Temple.

The next year, Temple built the two-story adobe that now houses the Rancho Los Cerritos museum. During his 20 years on the ranch, Temple raised two daughters and expanded the ranch's stock to 15,000 head of cattle and 30,000 sheep. He spent most of his time in the city of Los Angles managing the sale of meat, tallow, and hides. The day-to-day operation of the ranch was left to a foreman who had a reputation for being a mean character.

John Temple and his two daughters are buried on the ranch that today occupies only 4.7 acres. In the late '60s, Temple's grave was moved to make way for a freeway. It was then that strange things began to happen in the old adobe. Caretakers, museum docents, and visitors reported the ghostly image of a man that matched authentic photographs of Temple taken late in his life. Some have seen him with two children believed to be his daughters. When John Temple began making appearances at the house, lights flickered and disembodied footsteps would be heard on the second-floor hallway. Today, docents who work at the rancho museum dismiss the notion of a haunting. But ghost hunters and psychic investigators have identified at least four ghosts on the property. That is, human ghosts.

Outside the house, the distant sound of several small bells has been heard. The nature of this paranormal phenomenon puzzled ghost hunters until research revealed that many of the 30,000 sheep that roamed here wore bells. The meditation technique described in chapter 1 may enable ghost hunters to detect this imprint.

The ghost of the ranch foreman has been detected here too. Famed ghost hunter Richard Senate reported that psychics who visit this place were so shaken by the ghost's evil presence that they refused to make a followup visit to the site. Senate describes this ghost as an "evil force, bent on frightening people."

The power of this ghost was displayed for a séance group of ten people including a reporter and the museum director. While seated around a massive library table with their hands resting on its surface, these people felt the table rise off the floor then shift in the direction of a man whose comments irritated the ghost.

Ghost hunters who are looking for an encounter with something strange, powerful, and possibly evil might find Rancho Los Cerritos the perfect site.

THE GENERAL AND HIS CHILDREN

Banning Residence Museum
401 East M Street
Wilmington 90744
(310) 548-7777
www.banningmuseum.org

Twenty-one-year-old Phineas Banning arrived in California in 1851, penniless but full of ambition. When he died 34 years later, his list of accomplishments and accolades was matched by only a handful of the Golden State's pioneers. Banning saw great potential in the mud-choked port of San Pedro, dredged the channel, and created the Port of Los Angeles, expanding Southern California's world trade. He built a railroad, a telegraph system connecting San Francisco and Los Angeles, and a freight line to Salt Lake City, and provided land for the establishment of a military facility not far from his home. (See "Civil War Ghosts on Duty.") For his support of military development in the West, Banning was commissioned a general in the California militia.

Banning's elegant Greek Revival home in Wilmington overlooks the harbor he developed. Here he fathered eight children with his first wife, Rebecca Stanton. Five of the children died in this house, the last with Rebecca during childbirth. Banning's second wife, Mary Hollister, gave birth to three daughters but one died in infancy.

Phineas Banning's hard work, boundless ambition, and intelligence catapulted him to power and wealth, but he was no stranger to disappointment, failure, and tragedy. The emotional imprint of these moments of his life remain in his home, which is now a museum. In

The Banning Residence in Wilmington stands as a monument to Southern California pioneer Phineas Banning.

his study, ghost hunters have detected a thickened atmosphere and cold spots. Standing near the desk, sensitive visitors feel an invisible barrier as if Banning, or some other ghost, is denying access to his private space. A report posted on www.shadowlands.com states that Civil War generals have been seen in this room, planning military campaigns. This is probably erroneous and stems from a failure to understand that Phineas Banning's commission was granted without prior military education or training. Using modern vernacular, it was a status symbol granted as a kickback for giving 60 acres of land to the U.S. Army for one dollar. "General" Banning had nothing to do with planning military campaigns of the Civil War.

In the ornate dining room, the laughter of children has been heard when none are around. They move from one end of the room to the other, sometimes with disembodied footsteps. The large table was the scene of many happy family events. Visiting dignitaries and all the important people in Southern California dined here too.

Ghost hunters have visited the house in search of Phineas's first wife, Rebecca Stanton. It is believed she roams the second floor with her last baby in her arms.

GHOSTS OF THE BELOVED MANSION

Anaheim White House Restaurant
887 South Anaheim Boulevard
Anaheim 92805
(714) 772-1381
www.anaheimwhitehouse.com

This mansion, built in 1909 by Dosithe and Alberta Gervais, is now one of Southern California's best restaurants, the Anaheim White House Restaurant. Aside from its 12 charming dining rooms named for U.S. presidents, three-star cuisine, and celebrity patrons, several ghosts have been detected here. Such an intriguing combination led the Food Network to feature the White House Restaurant in a program about haunted restaurants.

As with most haunted places, a tragic event ties the spirits to this beautiful house. Sometime during the early decades of the 20th century, a young girl dashed into the street in front of the magnificent white mansion at 887 South Anaheim Boulevard. A passing truck hit the child. The shouting of other children at the scene attracted the mother's attention and she rushed from the house to her daughter's side. On seeing the gruesome injuries, she fainted. Neighbors carried the child into the house where, legend says, she died a short time later, surrounded by her grieving family.

This story has been retold so many times over the ensuing decades that the facts have become blurred. The known histories of the three families who occupied this house between 1909 and 1939 do not include the death of a little girl from a street accident. However, Robert Truxaw, age 17, was struck by a car while playing in the street. His injuries were not fatal.

Local historians speculate that the Waterman family, occupants of the home from 1916 to 1919, experienced the tragedy described by local legend. Their short occupancy leads to further speculation that they moved out rather than face continued reminders of the painful event. The Watermans are long gone, but the spirits of the little girl and her protective mother are still here. The pair often appears roaming the upstairs hallway and a room designated as the Blue Room. The woman is described as slim and beautiful with blond hair. She appears to be about 30 years old. Her little girl is about five years old. Both seem to be happy, walking hand-in-hand.

Restaurant owner, Bruno Serato, has also seen a female ghost believed to be the matriarch of one of the three families. Several restaurant patrons, too, have seen her. She is described as older and very pleasant. This ghost roams through rooms on both floors expressing satisfaction with the modern décor and the fabulous restaurant that now occupies her home.

Psychic investigators and ghost hunters have discovered the spirits of several children here. Their voices have been heard in the hallways, chandeliers swing and spin, objects move or disappear only to reappear at a surprising location. Disembodied footsteps are also heard as though children are running up and down the stairs. Door handles are turned by invisible hands.

In a room that was the Gervais family living room, a waiter encountered something he called a "wall of cold energy" that stopped him from moving. A visiting ghost hunter also felt this cold spot and interpreted it as a visit from Mrs. Louise Truxaw. With her husband, Dr. John Truxaw, she moved into the big white house in 1919 and raised eight children.

A COMMUNITY OF GHOSTS

Victorian Manor Tea Room
204 North Olive Street
Orange 92866
(714) 771-4044
www.victorianmanor.com

This charming Queen Anne Victorian house was built by William and Ella Granger in 1904. Today, it is a thriving tea room, luncheon café, and wedding facility that also offers a unique setting for private parties. Aside from all that, the Victorian Manor is also known as one of Orange County's most haunted sites.

For years, owners Jim and Carol Cox experienced doors that opened and closed by unseen hands, light bulbs that were removed from their sockets, cold drafts and icy spots, creepy feelings of being watched, and missing objects that turned up in another part of the house. Patrons also reported ghostly experiences. One customer sat down for tea and enjoyed a lively conversation with a charming lady in Victorian-era dress. Later, she learned that none of the living souls in the house were in costume and that her acquaintance was one of the ghosts of the Victorian Manor.

In March and September 2001, the Orange County Society for Psychic Research brought as many as 30 investigators to this location. This dream team of gifted psychics, historians, paranormal psychologists, and ghost hunters discovered a gathering of spirits that was truly amazing. William Granger and his son were discovered with a nanny named Rosalie and D. C. Pixley, a friend of the Granger family.

Several female spirits not related to the Granger family are here: two women named Hedda and Amber; Maryann Thomas, who likely died in 1926; a young woman in her wedding dress; an elderly lady with dark gray hair; and a woman known as Aunt Cora. A sad presence was detected by several psychic investigators that led to the discovery of the ghost of young "Emilie." Far along in her pregnancy, Emilie fell from the second-floor balcony and lost her baby. She recovered from her injuries, but she was so despondent that she killed herself.

Ghost children roam this old house, too, including a girl with curly blond hair and a little boy who likes to move silverware. Two boys, named Matthew and Erin, run through the house creating cold breezes. A little girl wanders in search of her Aunt Cora.

A Civil War veteran wanders, looking for his love, Wanda Olberg. Another man named Earl and a Mr. Utt show up on the veranda sometimes. Our psychic discovered the spirit of a woman who claimed she died in the September 11, 2001, attack on the World Trade Center in New York.

No explanation has been offered for the presence of so many

ghosts in one location. Most of them have no apparent connection with the house or the Granger family. They lived in various time periods, some predating the construction of the house. Others have taken up residence here, some distance from the location of their death.

THE CRAWFORD FAMILY GHOSTS

Rutabegorz Restaurant
264 North Glassell Street
Orange 92866
(714) 633-3260

This charming restaurant occupies a house built in 1915 for the Crawford family. Daniel and Annie Crawford ran a citrus farm and contributed to the local agricultural traditions of Orange County. They raised at least two children here, a boy and a girl, and left an indelible mark that has been noticed by succeeding occupants, including the proprietors and staff of various restaurants.

A family that lived here in the '50s became quite familiar with the ghost of a little boy believed to be Danny Crawford's son. The phantom boy became a playmate for two living children. He was most often seen in the kitchen.

The apparition of Annie Crawford has made appearances for decades. Described as sturdy-framed, she looks over restaurant patrons and kitchen staff while keeping an eye on the stove. She is often detected as a sudden gust of cold air or a chilling feeling that some invisible being is standing close by. Psychic investigators report that Annie generates an impression of a strong female presence as if she is trying to gain the attention of strangers in her house.

A male presence, though to be Danny Crawford, has been detected. He may be responsible for the malfunctioning of equipment such as the Coke machine, electrical failures, and doors that will not stay closed. One employee passed through a corridor and stepped around a man working atop a ladder. Thinking he was hired to help with renovations, the employee turned to take another look at the stranger only to see him, and his ladder, vanish. This man was probably Danny Crawford doing a little work on his house.

Danny and Annie Crawford have been sighted together. They walk arm-in-arm wearing period clothing. Sometimes, their muted conversations are heard. Sensitive visitors pick up on their voices and sense their presence as they enter the restaurant. The restaurant manager and staff seem to welcome these ghosts as well as ghost hunters who are looking for spirits and food.

PHANTOM MOVIE FAN

Warner Grand Theatre
478 West Sixth Street
San Pedro 90731-2632
(310) 833-8333
www.warnergrand.org

With a grand opening on January 20, 1931, this spectacular art-deco theatre welcomed movie fans during the golden age of film. Jack Warner called this opulent movie house "the castle of your dreams." Warner and his brothers (see "Ghost of Sam Warner," chapter 2) believed theatres such as this were the portals through which Depression-era moviegoers could escape their troubles and live their fantasies through the adventures and love affairs of big stars. They successfully sold this idea and made a fortune.

Famed architect B. Marcus Priteca designed this ornate theatre and its sister film palaces in Beverly Hills and Huntington Park. With fantastic interior features by designer A. T. Heinsbergen, the theatre is a time capsule of the moviegoing experience in the 1930s.

After the 1950s, the Warner Grand Theatre went through a 30-year decline, but was saved by the Grand Vision Foundation. After careful restoration, the theatre is now open and serves as a living museum of the golden age of film. The dead are known to join the Warner Grand supporters.

The ghost of a former employee likes to take a seat in the back row and enjoy a film. He creates cold spots and an icy feeling that suggest the empty seat is occupied. During a recent visit, a ghost hunter saw a shadowy figure seated with his right arm extended over the neighboring seat. When approached, the shadow vanished. A longtime resident

A phantom movie fan has been discovered at the 1931 Warner Grand Theatre in San Pedro.

of the neighborhood believes the back-row ghost is the spirit of a fellow who was a projectionist through the 1940s and early 1950s. This fellow was a devoted movie buff who spent many hours watching great films, over and over. In 1960, while screening *Spartacus,* he had a heart attack and died in the projection booth. Today, he leaves the projection equipment in the hands of others and enjoys the elegance and comfort of the Warner Grand Theatre.

MURDERED WAITRESS STILL ON DUTY

J J Live Oak Steak House
21700 Temescal Canyon Road
Corona 92883
(951) 479-0086

In 1988, a waitress named Michelle started working at a popular steakhouse on the edge of town. In a short time she became one of the favorites, showing a warm smile and maintaining a good attitude even when the restaurant was full of customers. Michelle often worked late at the steakhouse but she didn't mind because it became her social hub. Coworkers became her closest friends and late at night, when few customers were around, Michelle enjoyed hanging out with them in the kitchen, talking about the interesting people who had come through the restaurant that day and gossiping about mutual friends.

On the night of October 18, 1988, Michelle was one of the last to leave. As she walked across the dark parking lot behind the building, someone approached her from behind. Unconcerned with the rush of footsteps, she no doubt assumed it was the cook or dishwasher catching up with her for a final good-bye. Moments later, Michelle was dead. Her body was found days later, stuffed in the trunk of deserted car that had been sitting behind the restaurant for several weeks.

The man convicted of Michelle's murder is still in prison, but it is rumored that an employee of the steakhouse committed the crime. Some assume that fellow has moved on because Michelle has returned to work at the restaurant with that familiar smile and happy disposition.

The ghost waitress is known for flushing toilets at closing time, ringing the kitchen bell when orders are up, and helping the customers enjoy the special atmosphere of the J J Live Oak Steak House. Staff and customers have seen Michelle as a white, wispy shadow moving from the dining room to the kitchen area. Witnesses report that she is very nice, a little shy, and not scary.

There may be another ghost haunting the restaurant. A former owner named Larry shot himself in the office. People have reported the apparition of a man dressed in black who walks around the restaurant, including areas of the parking lot.

Standing in front of the steakhouse is an old twisted oak tree rumored to be a hanging tree. The restaurant stands on the site of a stagecoach depot established in the 1870s. In those days, the oak tree was a handy place to hang rowdy locals who harassed travelers, respectable ranchers, and businessmen. Some visitors to this site believe they can see an old hemp noose embedded in the tree bark. Not long ago, a ghost hunter visited the site and reported several cold spots and orbs around the tree. Psychic investigation produced a sense of profound sadness here.

CIVIL WAR GHOSTS ON DUTY

Drum Barracks Civil War Museum
1052 North Banning Boulevard
Wilmington 90744
(310) 548-2946
www.drumbarracks.org

Drum Barracks is the only original Civil War military facility remaining in the Los Angeles area. Built in 1862 and named for Adj. Gen. Richard C. Drum, the original barracks covered 60 acres and included the finest military medical facility west of the Mississippi River. Troops that trained here were charged with protecting Arizona Territory from Confederate intrusion. In 1862, 2,350 men marched from Drum Barracks to Santa Fe and fought in the western-most battle of the Civil War. Thousands of California volunteers passed through Drum Barracks on their way to regiments in the East. Many wounded veterans returned here for medical care that in most cases failed to save their lives.

Ghosts of Civil War veterans haunt this remnant of the largest military hospital in the West.

Today, modern homes now stand on most of the old camp's grounds, including the site of the military hospital. Though all that remains of this important military camp is a single two-story building that served as the junior officer's quarters, the Drum Barracks museum is supported by a dedicated staff and benefactors.

Drum Barracks is well known as a haunted site. A psychic investigation led by Barbara Connors identified several Indian spirits at the front of the building, a soldier with an injured foot, the spirit of a woman known as Maria, and a young boy. Other psychics and ghost hunters also detected the presence of these spirits. Historical records have confirmed such spirit discoveries.

It is well documented that Lt. Col. James Freeman Curtis, first commanding officer of Drum Barracks, lost part of his foot to frostbite. During his long residence here, he walked the grounds with a limp, creating a characteristic sound as he trod the wooden floors of the camp's buildings. Several people, including a man working as an exterminator, have seen this ghost. The colonel approached the man, asking for water and the whereabouts of the kitchen servant, Maria.

For years, the camp's western-most location led researchers to believe that Indians did not live here. But the discovery of obscure records confirmed Apache scouts from Arizona were indeed stationed here with U.S. troops. As for the spirit of a young boy detected by psychics, several people have heard his bouncing ball on the floorboards of the upstairs hall and bedroom.

Neighbors and passersby have seen a couple walking arm-in-arm on a second-floor balcony. Others have encountered a cold spot and a thick atmosphere in both the front courtyard and behind the structure. One longtime resident in the neighborhood told a ghost hunter that he believes his house sits on the site of the military hospital. The man admitted that he sees apparitions of men in his kitchen and garage. They appear for only a few seconds, but they are recognizable as Civil War-era soldiers.

If you visit Drum Barracks, ask the docents about a book containing records of paranormal events that occurred here. Over a 20-year period, a former museum director compiled hundreds of reports of strange phenomena and ghost sightings.

A GATHERING OF GHOSTS

Disneyland
1313 South Harbor Boulevard
Anaheim 92802-2309
(714) 781-4000
www.disneyland.com

The history of Disneyland and its founder is known throughout the world. The fantastic adventures, entertainment, opportunities for education, and dining experiences at Disneyland are unique. They reflect cartoon and film themes that have remained popular for 100 years or more. Walt Disney and his associates did indeed create the happiest place on Earth for children of all ages. Disneyland is a happy place for ghosts too. The place is loaded with them because a lot of people have lost their lives here, some from carelessness or their failure to follow park rules.

One of the most haunted places in Disneyland is the haunted mansion. If you talk to employees at this attraction late in the evening, when the crowds are gone, you might learn to recognize the fake ghosts from the real ones. Employees will tell you about a teenager who, amid grad night frenzy, stepped out of the "doombuggy" to get a closer look at the séance room. He stepped across the black-painted walkway, then fell 15 feet into a gap in the room's floor, breaking his neck. Since this tragic event, ghostly phenomena have occurred at the séance room on a regular basis. Strange sounds come from the walls, and icy cold spots appear with gusts of wind that come from various directions.

At the end of the ride, where visitors disembark from the doombuggies, employees often see a ghost dressed in a tuxedo. The ghost's features look real though his apparition is pale and thin. He appears in the mirror used to reflect the images of ghost caricatures. One employee felt this ghost's icy hand on her shoulder. This may be the ghost of a man who had a heart attack here in August of 1970 and died on the spot.

There is a story going around about a mother who requested permission from park officials to place her son's ashes inside the haunted mansion. She claimed he loved the attraction, visited it often, and had said he wished to reside there with the other ghosts. Of course, Disneyland officials refused her request. Trying to be true to her son's wishes, the woman concealed the ashes in a large purse, boarded a doombuggy, and in secret scattered her son's remains at various places within the mansion. It seems that the deceased boy's interest in the haunted mansion and his last wishes were misunderstood. Park employees and ghost hunters have seen a boy at the ride's exit sitting on the floor and crying. The appearance of this unhappy ghost has been interpreted as a sign that the boy did not want to be left at this site.

Another story about scattered ashes takes place at the Pirates of the Caribbean attraction. Once again, a well-meaning mother defied park officials and deposited her son's ashes at sites throughout the ride. This time, however, the child is elated to be enjoying his favorite Disneyland ride. His smiling ghost has been seen in the boats. This ghost has also been spotted on security monitors during test runs of empty boats. When ride operators check out the lone visitor, no one is found.

Elsewhere, a nineteenth-century photograph of a young woman hanging in the Christmas Shop may be haunted. People have seen a frown on her face that changes to a straight expression typical of the era. A gust of wind near the photograph changes direction when the woman's expression changes.

On Matterhorn Mountain people have reported the ghost of a woman named Dolly. Dolly either fell or jumped out of the bobsled only to be crushed by the following sled.

On Tom Sawyer's Island, two ghost boys have been seen dashing across the suspension bridge. At least three boys drowned in the Rivers of America near the island on grad night.

Ride operators have named the ghost that haunts Space Mountain, Mr. One-way. This fellow died here in the early 1970s after stepping out of the car midway through the ride and trying to walk back along the tracks. Perhaps he lost his hat or sunglasses and was trying to retrieve them. These days, Mr. One-way gets into cars that carry only one rider, but he disappears before reaching the end of the wild ride. He is described as a large man with red hair and a flushed face. This ghost also appears in the women's locker room.

Several other Disneyland ghost reports have been posted on Internet sites. These include the second floor of the firehouse on Main Street, It's a Small World, various sites in Tomorrow Land, the sailing ship *Columbia,* and the People Mover.

CORDELIA'S GHOST

Knott's Berry Farm
8039 Beach Boulevard
Buena Park 90620-3200
(714) 220-5200
www.knotts.com

Walter and Cordelia Knott arrived in Southern California in 1920 hoping to make a modest living by selling berries they planned to grow on a 20-acre farm. They ended up as founders of one of the southland's oldest and most popular amusement parks. Knott's Berry Farm was, for many years, the only place in Orange County to get a good meal and spend a few hours wandering through a fascinating collection of old western buildings Walter had relocated from ghost towns. Even when Disneyland opened, many people spent the day at the newer amusement park but drove up the road for a peaceful evening at Knott's Berry Farm. Part of the allure was Cordelia Knott's famous chicken dinner.

After opening the berry farm in 1928, the Knotts realized they needed something besides delectable fruit to draw customers. So, in 1934, Cordelia began serving home-cooked chicken dinners. They were such a hit that by 1937, the Knotts had to build a full-sized restaurant to accommodate people who drove from considerable distances. Often, crowds of people waited for an hour or more for a dinner in Cordelia's restaurant.

In order to keep people entertained during these long waiting periods, Walter moved the Old Trails Hotel from Prescott, Arizona, to Buena Park and established his famous ghost town. Within a few years several buildings from old western towns were added together with the complete rolling stock of the Denver and Rio Grande Rail Road and a replica gold mine. Cordelia's chicken dinners remained the prime attraction, but the Knotts ended up with a unique "ghost town" that included some modern rides, attractions, and shows.

Cordelia died April 23, 1974, leaving the management of the park in the hands of her children. According to people who work in the restaurant, Cordelia is still in charge of those famous chicken dinners.

Cordelia's ghost has been described as foglike but still recognizable as Mrs. Knott. She drifts through the restaurant looking at each table to see that the guests are satisfied. Her apparition is most often seen in one of the rear dining areas and the kitchen. Cordelia also casts ghostly shadows on the wall and creates the sound of her footsteps as she rushes through the various rooms of her famous restaurant. This ghost cannot part with the dream that became her life's work.

PHANTOM CYCLIST

Lynwood Park
Intersection of Martin Luther King, Jr. Boulevard and Bullis Road
(adjacent to St. Francis Medical Center)
Lynwood 90262
Lynwood Recreation Department
(310) 603-0220

In 2003, a young man cruised through the park on his mountain bike, enjoying the sunny day. Taking a turn through an area concealed by trees, he was attacked by two assailants. One of them drove a knife into his chest then inflicted several wounds to his neck and torso. The bloody crime scene was truly a mystery. There were no witnesses, no apparent motive, no connection between the victim and known criminals in the area, and no reason why such a gruesome killing should occur in broad daylight. Added to all of this, the murderers were never caught.

After an investigation that led nowhere, police concluded that the killing was a gang incident. Supposedly, one assailant was a gang leader while the other was a novice who committed the murder to earn his colors.

Not long after the murder, visitors to the park began to see odd things. At the site of the killing, fleeting shadows appeared, sometimes with a blur of color. At night, a small dot of light—an orb—hovered a few feet off the ground. Then, truly strange things began to happen. Regulars at the park reported seeing a cyclist pedaling along the bike path around a curve near some trees. If the cyclist approached a witness, he disappeared about 15 to 20 feet away. This apparition was partial but it was clear that the ghost was a young man riding a bicycle.

At the murder site, visitors reported seeing a man lying on the ground, reaching upward, beckoning for help. Again, this was a clear, partial apparition of a young man in great pain. These apparitions have been seen at all hours, day or night.

GHOSTS OF A MURDER-SUICIDE

K-Mart Store #7625
500 Carson Town Center
Carson 90745
(310) 533-0285

She was young—less than 20—and pretty. He was older and crazy in love. When he found her with another man, sharing an amorous moment in the stockroom of a large department store once known as Zodys, he went berserk. No explanation or pleading could quell his anger. He grabbed a box cutter left near a stack of cardboard and attacked the interloper. He slashed the man's neck and arms, opening his arteries. The girl stood frozen with fear as blood sprayed the walls of the stockroom and her casual lover fell to the floor. In an instant, the jealous boyfriend turned on his love and gave her the same treatment. In a few minutes she, too, lay dead on the stockroom floor. When the murderer caught his breath and saw the bloody bodies at his feet, he became so distraught that he opened his own arteries and joined his girlfriend in death.

This gruesome event tied the spirits to the death site and resulted in paranormal activity noticed by several employees long after the building changed hands and became a K-Mart. In fact, the ghostly activity became so scary that K-Mart hired paranormal investigators to find out why the stockroom and other parts of the store were haunted. This investigation discovered the three spirits of the murder-suicide and a fourth not connected with any event in the building's history.

Store employees have noticed icy spots, sudden cold breezes arising from open doors or windows, slamming doors, lights going on and off, and frequent feelings that some invisible person is standing close by. Several employees have seen a wispy apparition of a woman running across the stockroom. Some have heard her screams. The ghost of a man has also been seen at this location. He wanders about and appears confused by the things he sees. There are reports of a stockroom worker who was struck by a knife that flew cross the room, causing a large laceration. Falling boxes hit another employee.

The fourth spirit is believed to be a remnant of some event that occurred at this site before the store was built. This ghost is that of an older man dressed in rancher's clothing from the Spanish period. He has been seen in the aisles of the store late in the evening. A similar haunting has been documented in detail at the Toys "R" Us in Sunnyvale, California.

CHAPTER 5

Beach Cities

GHOST WAITRESS OF PARADISE COVE CAFÉ

28128 West Pacific Coast Highway
Malibu 90265
(310) 457-2503

The waitress is meticulous, arranging glassware, dishes, and silverware, closing doors, putting chairs in place, and walking through the café late at night to make certain everything is ready for the next day. Her dedication to her work is admirable, but a little spooky, because when she moves through the building she creates cold puffs of air, thickening the atmosphere just enough to make staff and customers wonder if something strange is happening. Well, something very strange is happening, because this waitress is dead. Local legend says that she died alone after working 30 years at the Paradise Cove Café.

To make matters more interesting, the ghost waitress is not alone in her work. A second spirit, probably a man, moves back and forth between the kitchen and dining room, turning lights off and on and opening doors. His movements are revealed by disembodied footsteps. On occasion, he calls out the names of employees, drawing their attention to some detail essential to excellent service.

Café employees have reported other creepy feelings when they work late at night. Footsteps and movement of objects have caused a few of them to head for the door without looking back.

Hauntings at this café are usually attributed to these spirits but there is another possibility. The café was constructed on the former site of a Native American village. In fact, many years ago, burial artifacts were uncovered here suggesting that the café sits on land that was once a Chumash Indian burial ground. It is possible that initial construction, and subsequent expansions, desecrated their graves, awakening spirits who now wander around the Paradise Cove Café.

INDIAN GHOSTS OF OLD HUMALIWO

Malibu Pier
Pacific Coast Highway
Malibu 90265
Pier Events office
(310) 456-8031

When the first Spanish explorers arrived at this magnificent spot on the coast in 1542, they found a large Chumash village spread across the mouth of the canyon and hundreds of Indians lounging on the warm sand near the surf. These peaceful, prosperous people called this place *humaliwo,* meaning "the surf sounds loudly." The Spanish adopted this word, but altered its pronunciation, leaving us with "Malibu." Today, this beach colony is home to the biggest stars in film and TV. Multimillion-dollar homes line the beach, surfers cut up the surf on the point, and sunbathers walk around hoping to see someone famous. Nothing remains to indicate the Indians were here for hundreds of years, except a few spirits who watch over humaliwo from a vantage point on the pier.

The Malibu Pier is a landmark dating from 1900. The Rindge family built the 780-foot pier to accommodate their fleet of yachts, and to provide their guests with a comfortable place to dine while enjoying the ocean breezes. In 1980, the pier became property of the State of California but later closed due to storm damage. After many years of renovation, the pier reopened in the summer of 2004. In spite of the improvements, spirits of the Chumash are believed to roam the long pier. A recent ghost hunt at this site revealed a partial apparition standing at the south rail of the pier midpoint in its length. The ghost hunter interpreted the ghost to be that of a Native American. Also, at the ocean end of the pier, in the south corner, they detected a thick atmosphere with a psychic impression of great sorrow and fear. They suspect that a murder or suicide took place here.

RESTROOM GHOST

Moonshadows Restaurant
20356 Pacific Coast Highway
Malibu 90265
(310) 456-3010

Moonshadows is one of the most romantic restaurants on the Pacific Coast Highway. Situated between the highway and the ocean, it affords diners an unparalleled view of beautiful blue water, breaking waves, and indescribable sunsets. Since 1971, this restaurant has been a favorite destination for locals and tourists. Some like the place

A ghost in the restrooms of Moonshadows Restaurant plays with water faucets.

and its charming Southern California beach atmosphere so much that death can't keep them away.

For many years people have reported water faucets in both restrooms at the Moonshadows Restaurant that turn on by themselves. Reliable witnesses told management that it isn't just a trickle of water. Hot and cold water run wide open. If you turn the water off then step into a stall, the water turns on again.

A ghost hunter who has been a frequent customer at Moonshadows observed the foggy outline of an old man in the mirror of the men's restroom. The image doesn't move. He stands facing the mirror, then fades away. There is no historical information available that would identify this ghost.

GHOST OF THELMA TODD

17575 Pacific Coast Highway
Pacific Palisades 90272
Death site nearby at 17531 Posetano Road

A movie star named Thelma Todd died on Monday, December 13, 1935, at the tender age of 30. Her death had all the elements of the classic Hollywood tragedy. She had starred in 108 films, opened a signature café on the Malibu coast, engaged in business with a shady, domineering character, and was often seen with gangsters. With such a tumultuous lifestyle, it wasn't a surprise that she was found dead, seated behind the wheel of her fancy car parked inside a locked garage. LAPD dismissed the case as a suicide by carbon monoxide poisoning. They said the talented young lady couldn't handle the pressures of her career, her business, and her difficult relationships. Many people bought this hasty conclusion, but others who have seen Thelma Todd's ghost wonder if there isn't something more to her tragic demise.

Numerous sightings of Thelma's ghost have awakened interest in her life and death and have brought to light much evidence that she was, in fact, murdered. When her autopsy report made its way into public hands, it revealed that she had suffered two broken ribs, a broken nose, multiple bruises, and strangulation marks around her neck. She even had suspicious bruises inside her mouth. When her body

The ghost of murdered silent-film star Thelma Todd cannot leave the art-deco building where she ran a famous café and nightclub in the 1930s.

was found on that Monday afternoon in 1935, she was wearing the same gown and $20,000 in jewelry that she had worn the preceding Saturday night. During the intervening 36 hours, two men had opportunity, capability, and motive to kill Thelma Todd.

Like many stars of her day, Thelma spent time with gangsters and others outside the movie business who had a glamorous mystique. On the Sunday prior to her death, Thelma was seen with New York crime boss Charlie "Lucky" Luciano. Lucky was in L.A. looking for locations to open illegal gambling operations. There were rumors that he had pegged Thelma's seaside café as the perfect location away from the bright lights of L.A. and Hollywood. Thelma teased Luciano a bit, played him along, but in the end, declined to get involved with his business. Hollywood legend tells us that Thelma had leaked information about Luciano's plans to the police. An informant inside the department tipped Luciano who, in turn, had Thelma silenced.

Another interesting theory concerns Thelma's partner in the Roadside Café, Roland West. It seems that West was an aggressive, domineering business partner who also had the hots for Thelma. She knew she had the upper hand with him, in everything, and walked out on him on a Saturday night while the café was full of customers. Witnesses claim that West yelled at Thelma as she slammed the door. Theorists believe West was tormented by Thelma's lack of interest in him. In a rage, he waited for her to return from the documented visit with Luciano late Sunday night. According to West's alleged deathbed confession, he confronted her at 3:30 A.M. Monday and tried to stop her from driving her car out of the garage, not to kill her. He claims he locked the garage door, leaving Thelma sitting in the car with the engine running. This confession failed to explain the injuries discovered at the autopsy.

Today, Thelma Todd roams the building that housed her signature café. Her apparition has been seen at the top of a stairway that leads to her former apartment. The movie star has also been seen outside the building under the arches of the main entrance. Some ghost hunters have reported paranormal activity in front of the garage in which she died.

This fascinating case needs more research by ghost hunters and psychic investigators. Contact with Thelma's spirit may identify her murderer.

ELEGANT GUESTS

The Georgian Hotel
1415 Ocean Avenue
Santa Monica 90401
(310) 395-9945
www.georgianhotel.com

This art-deco-style hotel was opened in 1933 and christened the Lady Windermere by her owner, Mrs. Rosamond Borde. Her vision was to create a hotel at the edge of the ocean as a retreat for the high society folks living in central Los Angeles. Of course, "high society" meant movie stars, directors, and producers with a few classy gangsters

Ghosts of elegant guests of this 1930s Santa Monica hotel mix with lively people from the film industry.

thrown in to make the place exciting. Frequent visitors included Carole Lombard, Clark Gable, Humphrey Bogart, Barbara Stanwyck, producer Frank Capra, and gangster Bugsy Malone. This clientele demanded the best and expected to find anything they wanted at the Lady Windermere, including hard liquor. Prohibition was in full swing throughout the U.S., but in the hotel's speakeasy, booze flowed like the tide in Santa Monica Bay. Big parties were frequent events, as were secret weekend getaways for big stars and their lovers. For two decades, this hotel was the hot spot on the west side of L.A. For many who stayed at the Windermere, rubbed elbows with the stars, and danced with glamorous underworld figures, the experience was the most exciting of their lives.

In the late 1950s, the hotel was sold, renovated, and reopened as the Georgian Hotel. Another round of renovations and upgrades made in 2000 restored the hotel's reputation for offering the best of any hotel in the southland. Political stars, movie stars, and directors such as Arnold Schwarzenegger, Meg Ryan, Tom Hanks, and Oliver Stone are among the Hollywood elite who have been seen at the Georgian, adding to the luster of this beautiful hotel. Others who add a special ambience to the hotel are from an older era.

Many hotel guests and staff have reported hearing disembodied voices at several locations, including the kitchen, bar, lobby, staircase, corridors on several floors, and patio. The voices of men and women are heard calling out, "Good morning," and "Hey, where're ya goin'?" The sounds of footsteps on hardwood floors—some made with high-heeled shoes—-have been heard in carpeted areas. Apparitions of people in clothing from the 1930s or 1940s have been seen dancing, drinking in the bar, or entering the restaurant. They appear solid and lifelike for a few seconds, then vanish. Music from these eras is also heard late at night. On the third and fourth floors, apparitions of females have been seen walking down the corridors and passing through locked doors to unoccupied rooms.

These paranormal events appear to be hauntings or emotional imprints on the environment made by people who loved the old Lady Windermere Hotel and had some of the best times of their lives here. Despite their death, they are enjoying the moment, over and over.

GHOST FISHERMAN OF SANTA MONICA PIER

200 Santa Monica Pier
Santa Monica 90401-3126
(310) 458-8900
www.santamonicapier.org/

This pier is a classic, oceanic pleasure lane extending far beyond the high-water mark on Santa Monica beach. Built in 1909, it affords visitors a chance to inhale fresh sea breezes before they are tainted with the typical L.A. air that sometimes overflows from the city onto the beaches. The salt air invigorates as the sound of breaking waves gives a little taste of the Southern California beach scene from a unique vantage point.

If Santa Monica pier looks familiar, it is because it has appeared in movies such as *The Sting, Falling Down, L.A. Story,* and *Forrest Gump.* It was also featured in several TV movies and programs, such as *Baywatch.*

The pier first opened as a Coney Island-style amusement park that included a grand carousel, shooting galleries, and a small Ferris wheel. In the 1920s, huge dance parties were held here, complete with dancers called flappers. In the 1930s and 1940s, many famous big bands made appearances, together with a few gangsters who dealt in contraband liquor. Since then, the old pier has gone through several periods of decline, decay, and renovation.

Regardless of its condition, amusements, or events, the pier has been in regular use by local fishermen for nearly 100 years. The fishermen are the early-morning crowd, standing at the rail, puffing on a cigarette, waiting for the big fish to bite. There are stories that tell of fishermen who were regulars on the pier for years until the day they disappeared leaving bait bucket and pole behind. Some of the old-timers believe these guys slipped over the rail into the sea, having had too many sips of brandy to ward off the chilly morning air. Others suspect a mugging that ended with an unconscious victim tossed to the waves.

What makes these stories a little creepy are the strange sounds sometimes heard at the far end of the pier. Visitors, including ghost hunters, have heard the disembodied sounds of a fisherman. These

The Santa Monica Pier has been a Southern California icon in movies and TV. Ghosts of old fishermen haunt the end of the pier.

sounds include the spin of the reel as a line plays out in a long cast, the muted rattle of bait buckets and other fishing gear, and the dull footfalls of someone walking in rubber boots. These sounds are no doubt hauntings or the imprint of pleasant times left behind by an old fisherman who now rests beneath the waves in Santa Monica Bay.

GHOST NUNS OF THE DORMITORY

Mount St. Mary's College
12001 Chalon Road
Los Angeles 90049
(310) 954-4000
www.msmc.la.edu

In 1927, the good Sisters of St. Joseph of Carondelet built a small liberal arts college in the Brentwood hills. Working long hours under traditional conditions of meager comforts, the sisters established an institution of higher learning that has granted more than 16,000 degrees. Today, Mount St. Mary's College stands among the better private college in Southern California, thanks to innovative academic programs and an excellent, dedicated faculty. Some of the teachers are so dedicated that they pass up retirement, even after their death.

In Carondelet Hall, phantom nuns walk the corridors of the dormitory keeping watch over the newer students, some of whom are living away from home for the first time. As many as three nuns, decked out in traditional habits, have been seen as partial apparitions. These hauntings have been reported on each floor of the building.

In Brady Hall, entire classes have witnessed the mystery of doors opening then slamming shut. Cold spots have been detected here as well as sudden gusts of wind. Psychic investigation revealed a sense of foreboding and extreme anxiety. Thick atmospheres have given some witnesses a perception of oppression.

Before the influx of Spanish explorers and settlers, Native Americans believed the Brentwood hills were home to great spirits. This invites the speculation that Brady Hall may sit on sacred ground or, at least, a burial site. If this is so, the building may be a disturbance to ancient spirits. Another possibility centers on outlaws, such as the infamous Tiburcio Vasquez, who roamed these hills in the 1840s and 1850s. There are stories of lost stashes of stolen gold guarded by the ghosts of outlaws. Such stories may provide an interesting approach to ghost hunts at this site.

ABBOT KINNEY, GHOST OF VENICE

Windward Avenue at Pacific Avenue
Venice 90291-5040
(310) 822-5425

By the age of 30, Abbot Kinney (1850-1920) had made his fortune by manufacturing cigarettes. Anxious to see the world, he breezed through every European capital and parts of South America before settling in Southern California's San Gabriel Valley in the early 1880s. His keen eye for lucrative businesses helped him find the coastal real estate market that offered room for big dreamers like himself. He envisioned not just a housing development, but an entire city on the coast of Santa Monica Bay.

Kinney's idea was to reclaim marshland and build a community styled after the Venetian Renaissance, including navigable canals. A tireless entrepreneur, he achieved his goal in astonishing time. On July 4, 1905, Venice of America was dedicated amid the cheers of 40,000 people. The city included homes and businesses, a few hotels, a 1,700-foot pier, and 16 miles of canals traveled by real Italian gondolas. The architecture was Venetian, complete with frescos, plazas, arcades, and tiled accents. Venice, as it was known, was connected to central Los Angeles by a railroad line that brought visitors, investors, and new residents. The community flourished in spite of problems with water circulation in the canals and poor attendance at lectures and concerts staged in the 3,600-seat auditorium.

After World War I, the charm and allure of Venice waned a bit as Southern Californians found other places to visit in their new automobiles. But on the eve of his death, on November 20, 1920, Kinney knew that Venice was an astounding success and a community that would endure the postwar changes sweeping across Southern California. However, only a month after Abbot's death, Venice began

The ghost of Abbot Kinney still walks the shaded paths of Venice, overlooking the canals he built as part of his grand dream.

to decline. A mysterious fire destroyed the dance pavilion and pier. Many of the smaller canals had to be filled in due to the terrible stench from stagnant water. Venice became a backwater to the rising sophistication of Los Angeles and Hollywood.

Abbot Kinney never gave up his love for the Venetian city he founded, even after his death. Today, his ghost walks the streets that lie over his former canals. He has been seen on Windward Avenue sporting a black top hat and formal clothing, strolling around the former Grand Circle of the canal system. He makes a regular pass along the Romanesque arcade at the intersection of Windward and Pacific Avenues, which was once the heart of his community. There are reports of his partial apparition on Venice Way, Grand Boulevard, and Canal Street. Some witnesses have seen only Kinney's tall boots, cane, or cape moving in silence past the canals.

INDIAN SPIRITS OF PLAYA VISTA

Vicinity of Culver and Lincoln Boulevards in Playa del Vista, north of Los Angeles International Airport (LAX)

Centuries ago, a great village known as Washna stood on this land. The homes, cemeteries, and large ceremonial centers of the Gabrielino-Tongva Indians occupied hundreds of acres. Bordered on the north by marshlands that became Marina del Rey, the Westchester bluffs to the east, and beaches to the west, these thriving Indians established an important center for trade with other villages, including the Indians of Santa Catalina Island. Spanish explorers found well-built houses, large canoes, and many tools, weapons, and farming implements. When the missions were established, many Indians from Washna were "recruited" by mission fathers to work as farmers, artisans, and builders and to tend livestock.

The intrusion of Spanish, Mexican, and American settlers dissipated this culture. By the mid-1850s, only a few huts remained at Washna. By 1875, native grasses and shifting sands covered ceremonial sites and cemeteries, and the overflow from the nearby Ballona Creek created wetlands. For almost 100 years, this area remained open ground, wind-blown and overcast with marine air, dotted in some places by groups of houses perched on high ground.

Housing developments slowly encroached on the land until the 1990s, when this choice piece of ground, situated between LAX and glamorous Marina del Rey, was selected for the construction of luxury houses and condominiums, professional offices, and at least one major hotel. An army of construction workers, operating huge earth-moving equipment, broke ground that had not been disturbed since the days of the Tongva. That is when the trouble started.

Construction crews excavating a drainage ditch uncovered human remains identified as Native American. These graves also contained jewelry and other burial artifacts. At first, consulting archeologists and local Indian leaders assumed these few graves were the extent of the burials in the area. But research, and additional discoveries, made it clear that Playa Vista was a major archeological site. Construction resumed with caution, as several hundred additional graves were found.

Disturbance of these graves may be linked to strange mists that have been seen in the area. Small blue clouds float a foot off the ground and rise to a height of about four or five feet. At times they are stationary but sometime they move, slowly, against the wind. Some people have seen lights, described as orbs, at night. There are reports of electrical and mechanical problems with some of the construction equipment too. It is anticipated that occupants of several new homes and offices in this development will experience paranormal activity linked to the desecration of Indian graves. Access to the Playa Vista area is limited due to continued construction, but ghost hunters can visit the grounds occupied by the Tongva by way of streets that include Vista del Mar (from Culver Boulevard), Falmouth Avenue (off West Manchester Avenue), and Veragua Drive (off West 80th Street).

GHOST BODY SURFERS

King Harbor Breakwater, near King Harbor Yacht Club
280 Yacht Club Way
Hermosa Beach 90277-2091
(310) 376-2459

A massive rock breakwater protects this magnificent yacht harbor, filled with some very expensive nautical toys. The breakwater runs several hundred feet outward from the beach before making a 90-degree left turn to parallel the coast. On its seaward, or outer side, big waves sometimes break close to the rocks as the swells run toward the Chart House Restaurant situated on the beach. On big surf days, the breakwater is a challenging place for accomplished body surfers. For those less skilled in this hazardous sport, the powerful surf and sudden changes in the swells can be deadly. More than a few surfers have hit the rocks, suffering serious injuries. A few have had the ride of their life—the last ride of their life.

Two apparitions seen here may be the ghosts of surfers who lost their lives on the King Harbor rocks. One body surfer, wearing a black full-body wetsuit, streaks across the front of a breaking wave only to disappear a few feet from the rocks. Another appears after sunset. This partial apparition is a young man with long blond hair, sitting on the rocks above the waterline where the breakwater turns to parallel the coastline. He gazes at the breaking waves, perhaps waiting for the surf to rise before entering the water.

JAKE, THE HIGH-SCHOOL GHOST

Redondo Beach Union High School
631 Vincent Park
Redondo Beach 90277-3125
(310) 798-8665

For years, the ghost of a high-school student named Jake has been seen here. Jake died on campus in the 1940s by mysterious means. One story describes Jake as a nice kid who got involved with a girl who was the sweetheart of a Marine. When the Marine came home from World War II after fighting in the Pacific, friends told him about Jake's romance with his girl. He became enraged, cornered Jake in the boys' restroom, and beat him to death. There are reports that the tile grout is still stained with Jake's blood. Others place the site of death in the auditorium.

Whatever the cause of Jake's demise, he still hangs out at this beach-city high school. By all reports, he is a noisy ghost who creates paranormal activity at several sites, including knocks on the walls, lights turning on and off, and the sudden appearance of objects lost weeks or months earlier. Jake's partial apparition has been seen in the auditorium and on the stairs leading to the projection booth. Several students and teachers have detected cold spots here. At times, distant laughing is heard, and paper airplanes appear out of nowhere, floating to the floor of the auditorium. Jake also appears in the main corridor near the boys' restroom and near the principal's office.

There are reports that Jake is not alone. Another man died a few years ago in the auditorium. He suffered a heart attack, died on the spot, and now creates creepy atmospheres at the death site. It would be interesting to investigate interaction between this spirit and Jake.

California state law requires that all visitors to public schools must check in at the office, present identification, and obtain a visitor's pass.

GHOSTS OF PORTUGUESE BEND

Portuguese Bend
Access the coastal walkway at Cherryhill Lane
Palos Verdes Peninsula 90274

From the early 1820s to the late 1840s, ships from American East Coast ports stopped at this section of California beach to deliver goods ashore and to take on a cargo of hides gathered from the missions and ranchos of the Los Angeles region. This commerce used lifting gear to transport goods to and from the beach as well as several rough warehouses built on the plateaus a short distance from the cliffs. Sailors carried the heavy loads between small boats waiting beyond the surf and the rocky beach. One of these sailors, Richard Henry Dana, described details of the work in the 1836 American classic *Two Years Before the Mast*. Dana often remarked about the desolation of the peninsula, the brooding cliffs, and the strange atmosphere of the rocky beaches. During the months he was stationed here, living alone in a shack overlooking Portuguese Bend, Dana saw strange lights and odd mists that were not typical of sea spray, marine air masses, or fog.

Modern visitors to Portuguese Bend have reported orbs and other lights, mists on the beach, cliffs that roughly approximate the dimensions of a man, and disembodied voices. The voices call out orders and seek to get attention. One ghost hunter heard, "Hey you, over

Shipwrecks and other tragic events at Portuguese Bend left several ghosts on the cliffs overlooking the Pacific Ocean.

here. Over here, now!" An immediate search of the area turned up no other living soul.

Several visitors have reported seeing apparitions of drowned SCUBA divers, sailors on the rocks below the cliffs, and old sailing ships anchored just beyond the surf line. Sailors and old ships may be hauntings or environmental imprints from the days of Richard Henry Dana. It is unknown how many divers have lost their lives or escaped harrowing experiences in the waters of Portuguese Bend. There seem to be a few who remain here, awaiting rescue.

SPIKE, HAUNTED GROUND

Vacant lot between Main Sail Drive and Burma Road (access from Ladera Linda Park) in the Portuguese Bend region
Rancho Palos Verdes 90274

Local legend tells of a teenage axe murderer who did away with his entire family. The family lived in a house near Lunada Bay. When the crime was discovered, the walls and floors of the small house were covered with blood and human tissue. A fire later destroyed the building, leaving scorched ground and a crumbling foundation. Today, vegetation has grown over the murder site, and the lot that remains vacant is regarded as haunted. Locals refer to the place as "Spike."

Over the years, several people have tried to build a dream house here, but various problems led to failure. Noxious odors, strange lights, and a sickening feeling leading to severe nausea are just a few of the problems people encountered.

Ghost hunters visiting the site have heard screams and seen the apparition of the house in which the murders occurred. The structure appears in a fog, then fades away. Psychic investigations turned up a deep sense of sadness, fear, and anger. Others have reported electrical problems and sudden engine failure with their cars if they stop near this site.

A review of *Los Angeles Times* archives did not turn up reports of a mass murder at this location, but archive searches often fail to uncover stories. It is possible that the alleged murders occurred several decades ago and did not make the pages of the newspaper.

THE LADY OF THE LIGHT

Point Vicente Lighthouse
Palos Verdes Drive and Los Verdes Boulevard
Palos Verdes Peninsula 90274

It seems that every old lighthouse has a ghost story attached to it. These stories are often spawned by common elements, which include a remote location, dangerous sea conditions nearby, wind-swept cliffs and pounding surf, many years of lonely vigil by a dedicated keeper-of-the-light, and, sometimes, decades of sacrifice by a devoted wife. All of these can be found in the history of Point Vicente Lighthouse. But the place is no longer remote. The communities of San Pedro and Palos Verdes have grown to the very edge of the lighthouse grounds.

Point Vicente Lighthouse is haunted by a lady who became lost in a fog and fell to her death from the nearby cliff.

The pounding surf and wind-swept cliffs are still there, though, giving visitors some idea of the nearby danger.

In fact, the ghost of Point Vicente Lighthouse was a victim of those dangerous cliffs. The tall woman with long hair and flowing gown is believed to be the ghost of a light keeper's wife. It is said that she enjoyed daily walks along the path that followed the edge of the cliffs. Under the Southern California sun, these walks among wildflowers and alongside the beautiful blue waters of the ocean restored her spirits. One day, a sudden fog rolled in and she became disoriented. Losing sight of the path, she fell hundreds of feet to her death on the rocks awash by crashing surf.

The lady of the Point Vicente Lighthouse is still there, seen most often at night in the space between the lighthouse and the cliffs. She is reported to be a wispy, partial apparition, but some ghost hunters have seen her complete, quite solid apparition. There are reports that this ghost has been detected inside the lighthouse as well. Her appearance is often preceded by a cold gust of air and sudden change in the atmosphere.

CHAPTER 6

Nearby Communities:
Santa Barbara to San Diego

Within two hours' travel time from Los Angeles are many popular destinations for day trips or weekend getaways. Many of these locations, such as the charming Santa Barbara area, Catalina Island, and San Diego, have a rich historical legacy preserved in old public buildings, houses, inns, cemeteries, ships, and numerous sites of historic events. Check with a local visitor's bureau or historical society to get a map of historic sites and information about events such as special tours, festivals, and anniversaries of events that may be linked to ghostly activity.

THE ROBED GHOSTS

Mission Santa Barbara
2201 Laguna Street
Santa Barbara 93101
(805) 682-4713
www.sbmission.org/home.html

The proud queen of the missions, founded in 1782, still sits upon her high throne, commanding a fantastic view of the city and distant ocean. Since she was constructed of quarried sandstone, instead of the usual adobe, her beauty has withstood time. There were events, though, that placed her in jeopardy. An Indian uprising in 1824 and a soldier revolt in 1830 brought violence to her doors and marked the Greek facade with bullet holes. But the selection of Mission Santa Barbara in 1834 as the residence of the first bishop of

Mission Santa Barbara is known as the queen of the California missions.

California protected her against the looting and destruction that ruined many other missions.

Today, the clanging bells in the twin Spanish towers can be heard everywhere in Santa Barbara. When they sound, time seems to stand still, and the locals listen with awe, amazed at something that has continued without interruption since the mission's dedication in 1820.

Each day hundreds of tourists visit the mission, flowing in and out of its sanctuary, which is still an ordained Catholic church with a dedicated congregation. The remaining parts of the original mission, including a kitchen, dining hall, library, and sleeping quarters for the padres, are decorated with artifacts from the 1820s and 1830s to represent early mission life. During the day, throngs of tourists provide inescapable reminders of the present that softens the atmosphere of the past. But at day's end, the long shadows of time can be seen stretching across the grand steps, filling the arcade with darkness and chilling the air over the cemetery.

The cemetery located on the east side of the mission is almost always dark and cold. Tall trees and the mission's walls block out the sun most of the day. Lingering shadows seem to slow the passage of time, creating a heavy atmosphere laden with strange scents. Cries of peacocks sometimes pierce the air. This cemetery contains more than 150 fascinating headstones, but the unmarked graves of 5,000 Indians fills the area with apparitions, strange sounds, cold spots, thick atmosphere, and the peculiar sense that someone is touching or watching you.

Ghost hunters have reported sighting robed figures similar to those seen at many of California's Spanish missions. The apparitions of monks or church padres appear most often at the far end of the cemetery, next to the east wall of the mission. Two nuns have been sighted near this spot as well. Reports of a phantom baby crying aroused the interest of famed ghost hunter Richard L. Senate. Audio recordings made in the cemetery revealed only the baying of peacocks.

A tall male apparition appears at several locations within the cemetery, including near the *lavada* in front of the mission. He has long black hair and a brown face and generates the impression of great power. He might be the spirit of a military leader or an outlaw denied burial at the mission.

THE LADY IN WHITE

Santa Barbara Community College
761 Cliff Drive
Santa Barbara 93109-2794
(805) 965-0581
www.sbcc.net

The Lady in White walks along the edge of a bluff near the Winslow Maxwell overlook an hour or so after sunset. In the darkness, her long white dress and shawl move with the wind, making her appear more like a cloud floating inches off the ground than a young woman. She seems anxious, as though she is searching for someone. While taking in the sweeping view of the coastline, wide beach, and placid waters below the bluff, she disappears in a misty cloud of blue light.

The ghost woman walks the grassy site on the Santa Barbara Community College (SBCC) campus where a small Spanish fort was erected over 200 years ago. The guns at this position commanded the approach to Santa Barbara, protecting it from pirates, foreigners, and Indian bands that opposed the rule of the mission fathers. The garrison of troops assigned here lived nearby with their families, but long periods of separation were common. Soldiers remained at their posts for several days before receiving a short leave. Their wives faced incredible hardships, endured the discomforts of crude homes, and faced the uncertainties of military duty at the farthest outpost of Spain's empire. It is no wonder that their days were filled with anxious moments while their loved ones were at their posts.

Two legends offer limited information about the ghost lady of SBCC. Some ghost hunters believe she was an Indian killed by raucous Spanish soldiers. No explanation has been offered to explain why the anxious ghost would revisit the site of her murder, seemingly searching for someone. Witnesses report that her gown does not resemble the dresses worn by local Indian women. Many believe she is a Spanish woman who died in childbirth at the nearby presidio. After her death, and the death of her child, she went in search of her husband, seeking his comfort. Perhaps she never found him and that is why she still walks the bluff overlooking the Santa Barbara harbor.

THE THREE NUNS OF ORTEGA ROAD

Ortega Ridge Road at Highways 101 and 192
Montecito 93108-26210

The pain and horror is still there, a lasting emotional imprint on old Ortega Ridge Road, south of Santa Barbara. The peace that came with death is there, too, along with the forgiveness granted by the victims. Many people who visit the site of the Three Nuns Massacre feel these things. A few have seen the three sisters, known as Las Tres Hermanas, their shining faces and heavenly blue eyes shrouded by flowing black habits.

The area through which Ortega Road passes was once dotted with small Indian villages. These villages were not part of the Mission Santa Barbara community. In fact, many of the Indians who lived in the area rebelled against the rules and laws of the mission fathers and kept to themselves. Indians, brandishing weapons and threatening attacks, often followed soldiers and priests who passed through the area. Sisters from the mission ignored the threats and reached out to the Indians by treating the sick and offering other comforts.

Local legend tells of three nuns who entered the area during a time of fierce revolt against three Southern California missions, probably in 1824. In spite of warnings not to leave Santa Barbara, the nuns journeyed up the winding road carrying medicine, clean bandages, and candles. Before they reached the first village, the nuns were captured by a band of Indians who tortured, molested, and killed them, then mutilated the bodies. The story of this awful crime spread through the region with an interesting footnote that before losing consciousness, the sisters forgave their murderers.

Within days of the murders, local Indians reported seeing the three nuns standing at the site of the massacre. To this day, travelers on Ortega Road see the three nuns at the roadside. They stand with their arms folded within their black habits. Their bright blue eyes and white shining faces seem to glow in the night. They turn as travelers pass by, then disappear into the night. Daytime sightings are rare, but the emotional imprint of the murders can be detected anytime.

HECTOR AND THE HOUSE OF SPIRITS

The Big Yellow House
108 Pierpont Avenue, P.O. Box 779
Summerland 93067
(805) 969-4889

When driving north from Los Angeles to Santa Barbara, it is almost impossible not to notice a big yellow house perched on a hillside next to the freeway as you pass through Summerland. The building stands out from its surroundings and attracts a lot of interest in its architecture, but many visitors to the area, and residents of

Southern California, zip by at freeway speeds, promising themselves to stop sometime. On future trips, when these busy travelers do stop at the Big Yellow House restaurant, they are amazed to find much more than great food and a fascinating history. The resident ghost, Hector, may turn a relaxing meal into the adventure of a lifetime.

The big house was built in 1884 by a spiritualist, Henry L. Williams, who came to the sunny shores of the Pacific Ocean from the stifling climate of the East Coast. He found paradise along the coastline between Santa Barbara and Ventura in a hamlet called Ortega. Amazed at the mild year-round climate, he renamed the little town Summerland and established a spiritualistic community. The big house was to be a center of learning, séances, and a gathering place for like-minded people who were fascinated by the spiritual world. But Henry's ambitions were short-lived. He died in 1899 by falling into an oil well on his property. Henry's widow wasted little time. She married a wealthy oil man, a Mr. Becker, and remodeled the house, making it the showplace of the coast. Becker died in 1932, followed by Mrs. Becker two years later. The elaborate mansion stayed in the family until 1974, when it was converted into a restaurant.

Now, the Beckers are gone, but it seems that at least one ghost who attended the séances years ago has stayed on. Famed ghost hunter Richard Senate and his team of paranormal investigators journeyed to the Big Yellow House and identified several spirits who wander through the restaurant creating cold spots and sudden breezes.

The restaurant staff has had some fantastic experiences with a spirit they call Hector. Hector is a prankster who opens and closes windows, plays with lights, smashes dishes, and even grabs the skirts of waitresses as they pass. This ghost works at his haunting. One morning the manger arrived to find that Hector had stacked all the tables on top of each other. On each table were four place settings in perfect order. In contrast to this meticulous haunting, Hector has also spent a good portion of the night smashing dishes and glassware.

There is reason to believe that Hector died in the house of cardiac arrest. A medium with Senate's paranormal investigators entered a trance and spoke with a strained, raspy voice as the room's temperature dropped. Speaking through the medium, the spirit complained of chest pain then stopped communicating.

Several teams of investigators have studied paranormal activity at the Big Yellow House. A group from UCLA recorded a great deal of activity and classified this building as "very" haunted.

A HOTEL FULL OF GHOSTS

Pierpont Inn
550 Sanjon Road
Ventura 93001
(805) 643-6144
www.pierpontinn.com/

The Pierpont Inn is one of those rare businesses in California that has remained in the hands of one family for more than 70 years. Austen Pierpont built the original inn in 1910. He managed the establishment only three years before moving on to become an architect. The inn changed hands a few times until 1928, when it was purchased by descendents of Ventura pioneers Gus and Mattie Gleichmann. Ownership and management have remained within the Gleichmann family through several renovations that included significant additional construction. The personal dedication of succeeding generations is a key element in the Pierpont's lasting success. The personal attention of former generations may play a role too. The ghosts of some of them are still there, watching over things to make sure all is well at the Pierpont Inn. In fact, this inn may be one of the most haunted on the California coast.

Much of the ghostly phenomena reported by the restaurant staff members occur in areas not accessible by guests of the inn. In offices, workspaces, the kitchen, and the back bar, mists appear then disappear and gusts of wind come out of nowhere. Cold spots are felt. Some staff have heard phantom footsteps, the ruffling of Victorian dresses, and locked doors opening and closing. Full apparitions have appeared as well. Late one night, in an office that had been guestroom number 6, the night auditor looked over the day's receipts with another woman. Without a sound, a well-dressed man entered the room and sat down. Stunned, one of the women asked him what he wanted. A moment later, the man disappeared. When the women got over the shock, the auditor realized the gentleman was Ted Gleichmann, a former owner and manager of the inn, who died in 1975.

In the dining room and bar, strange mists appear, often floating over a table. The restaurant's staff are used to the phenomena. Often, something more solid appears. Staff members and customers have seen a man in horn-rimmed glasses dressed in a wrinkled brown suit pass through these areas, looking things over, checking the doors. This ghost is Gus Gleichmann, conducting his rounds just as he did every night before his death in 1938.

In the bar, in hallways, near the pool, and within the lower parking area, men, women, and children dressed in Victorian or Edwardian period clothing are often seen as partial apparitions. These former guests of the inn sometimes acknowledge a shocked staff member or customer and invite him to follow.

While working late at night, a houseman and his assistant encountered two ghosts in the Anacapa/Marine banquet room. While working at a table, the assistant saw a man and a woman walk across the room and sit down nearby. In moments, the couple disappeared. After shaking off the experience, the men moved on to work in the adjoining San Miguel room. When the assistant entered the room, he found the tables covered with food and drinks. It was filled with people, too, including the ghostly couple seen earlier in the Anacapa room. They motioned to the assistant to join them. As he watched, shaken to his toes, everyone in the room disappeared.

One guest complained to the front desk one night that the noisy party in the adjacent room made sleep impossible. She and her companion reported singing, music, loud voices, horns and noisemakers, and the sound of dancing. This was a veritable New Year's Eve party, except the month was May. The night manager went to the room to quell the party but found that it was empty. There was no sign that anyone had been in the room since it was checked by the house staff earlier in the day.

Guests in the rooms of the East Wing experience quieter ghosts. Draperies sway then fall into place, lights go on and off, and cold spots appear. Some of these ghostly activities have been investigated by ghost hunter Richard Senate and presented on the Travel Channel. There is no explanation for the large number of ghosts at the Pierpont Inn. Good food and drink and comfortable accommodations at a beautiful location next to the ocean may be irresistible to some spirits, just as it is to the living.

GHOST OF THE SUICIDE LOVER

Landmark No. 78 Restaurant
211 East Santa Clara Street
Ventura 93001
(805) 643-3264
www.landmark78.com/

About 1900, an Italian immigrant, Carlo Hahn, moved his family to the quaint town of Ventura, seeking the American dream. Adopting the traditions of his new country, Carlo went into business with another Italian transplant named Giovanni Ferro, purchased a home, and increased the size of his family. After a few years of hard work, business started to turn a nice profit, so Carlo moved a short distance across town into a two-story Victorian house that now houses the Landmark No. 78 Restaurant.

Carlo liked the customs of his new country, but when it came to his family, he followed old-world traditions. He arranged for his daughter, Rosa, to marry a man much older than she, in all likelihood, one of his business associates. Rosa honored her father's wishes but dreaded entering a loveless marriage. Apparently she grew quite depressed and lonely after her wedding. Her husband left her alone for weeks at a time and paid little attention to her when he was home.

Then, a young Italian boy in the neighborhood attracted Rosa's attention. They started with innocent visits, but it wasn't long before they became lovers. Shortly after that, Rosa discovered she was pregnant. Her husband was furious and chased the boy out of town, as far as San Francisco, where he disappeared. Humiliated, Rosa returned to her father's house, walked upstairs to a quiet room, and hung herself.

Rosa is still there, in Carlo Hahn's house on Santa Clara Street. It is said that she is a playful ghost, turning lights on and off, closing doors, locking windows, creating cold spots, and unnerving restaurant staff and customers with phantom footsteps and that creepy feeling that an invisible person is watching. But psychics and ghost hunters who have investigated the haunting report that Rosa's ghost projects a profound sense of sadness as she moves about the house. The women's restroom on the second floor is filled with an energy described as thick or heavy, possibly reflecting Rosa's misery. Legend says that she committed suicide in this small room.

The ghost of Rosa Hahn has been seen in a mirror on the second floor. She appeared in a Victorian dress, and her neck was described as elongated, possibly the result of her hanging. Rosa has been seen at the top of the stairs as well. Several witnesses have reported seeing a full-body apparition wearing a red, blue, or green dress. In the red room, a banquet hall on the second floor, a strange presence is felt. This may have been Carlo's bedroom. No doubt Rosa Hahn remains in her father's home, seeking forgiveness and the comfort of her childhood surroundings.

GHOST OF SYLVIA MICHAELS

Bella Maggiore Inn
67 South California Street
Ventura 93001
(805) 648-0277

Some say she was a prostitute who never found a way to get out of the oldest profession. Instead, Sylvia Michaels sank lower, suffering mental and physical abuse while others around her hit the high road to success in the flush times after World War II. Others say she was a writer who spent time in dirty bars and brothels gathering material for her books. Whatever her occupation, Sylvia Michaels slipped into the dark side of life from which she never escaped.

In 1947, Sylvia was alone, despondent, and probably ill. Concluding that her life was a miserable failure, she climbed the steps to her room, number 17, in the downtown hotel. She locked the door, emptied the closet of her meager possessions, entered the small space, and shut the closet door. In the darkness, she placed a belt around her neck and hung herself from the hanger bar.

A few years later, things started to happen at the hotel, by then named the Bella Maggiore Inn. Disturbances described as "poltergeist" events became more frequent and terrifying for the hotel staff and guests. By the early 1990s, the Bella Maggiore had a reputation as a haunted inn. Ghost hunters and psychics were called in to investigate, and a documentary for TV was taped.

Psychic investigations revealed that Sylvia Michaels was behind many of the strange happenings at the inn that included objects thrown across a room, buzzing in visitors' ears, the appearance of strange balls of light, the odor of rose-scented perfume, and a phantom performance on the piano. A psychic who also sensed a profound sadness heard the sound of a woman sobbing on the second floor near room 17.

Ghost hunters have reported movement of closet doors and a sudden drop in room temperature. Others have seen the apparition of Sylvia Michaels and heard her speak. She often appears as a tall, human-shaped body of light. One ghost hunter saw the apparition of a woman in lifelike detail standing near her bed.

Other ghosts have been identified in the Bella Maggiore Inn. Sometime in the 1960s a man named Mark died of a drug overdose somewhere on the second floor. A little girl, Elizabeth, was murdered on the ground floor in the 1930s. A fourth spirit, identified through a séance, is an unpleasant man who is supposed to growl then laugh. This ghost may be the phantom piano player.

THE DARK LADY

Olivas Adobe
4200 Olivas Park Drive
Ventura 93005
(805) 654-7837
www.olivasadobe.org/

Don Raimundo Olivas grew wealthy during the gold rush of 1849 and the 1850s. Cattle from his rancho in Ventura were driven north twice a year to feed the 300,000 miners who roamed the Sierras, gathering the gold, founding new towns, and starting families. As the money came in, Don Raimundo improved his rancho with more outbuildings, beautiful gardens, and a two-story hacienda to house his wife, Dona Teodora, and their 22 children. Fiestas were frequent events at the Olivas hacienda, with food, wine, music, and games that went on for days. Times were good and the Olivas family became well known in the region. The wealth of Don Raimundo became well known too.

One night in 1855 a gang of bandits rode onto the rancho, firing their guns and driving the Mexican cowboys into a pen. They ransacked the house, searching for $75,000 in gold coins rumored to be hidden there by Don Raimundo. Their search turned up only a little money and a few silver candleholders. Angry and disappointed, the bandits ripped Dona Teodora's gold earrings from her ears, killed her, and then shot several others before they made their escape. The bandits rode away, but a posse followed and captured some of the outlaws. A nearby tree and a rope delivered swift justice.

There are various accounts of that terrible night in 1855 that may shed light on the haunting at the Olivas Adobe. One legend says that Don Raimundo saw the bandits approaching and gave his strongbox of gold coins to a trusted servant to bury. In the melee, the servant was shot and unable to reveal the location of the strongbox before he died. Over the years, treasure hunters have sought Don Raimundo's gold, but it has not turned up, yet.

It is suspected that one of the ghosts of the Olivas Adobe is the servant. He appears in the corner of the courtyard near an old graveyard that has been covered for decades. Ghost hunters believe the ghost of Don Raimundo is also in the courtyard. He may be searching for the hidden gold or watching for the return of the bandits. His emotional imprint from the night of the attack on his hacienda, made stronger by the loss of his wife, is detectable by those who can get in touch psychically with 1855.

The most frequent ghost at the Olivas Adobe is the Dark Lady. She appears in the kitchen, living room, and sewing room and on the balcony. Psychic investigators feel tension and anger in the air when she is present. The ghost is believed to be Dona Teodora, known as the

Dark Lady because she is wearing a black dress and her black hair falls over her shoulders.

Several explanations have been offered for Dona Teodora's haunting of the hacienda. She may be searching for her children or her husband's gold, or she may be seething with anger that she was murdered and her home ransacked by a mob of thieves. Whatever her reasons, her emotional imprints are strong and her presence is experienced often by visitors to the Olivas Adobe.

THE GHOST MONK

Mission San Buena Ventura
211 East Main Street
Ventura 93001
(805) 643-4318

It seems that every California mission has at least one ghost story, perhaps because life at the missions was hard, often ended too soon by illness, accident, or the occasional skirmish with renegade Indians or bands of outlaws. The mission fathers lived and worked at the very edge of civilization, often cut off from neighboring missions for months at a time. They got by with meager supplies and faced the monumental tasks of constructing the mission church and other buildings. In addition, they converted the Indians to Catholicism and established viable farms. At the same time, the mission Indians suffered the rapid dissipation of their culture, the ravages of "white man's" diseases, and the harsh conditions as laborers and farmers. It is no wonder that the thousands who died at the missions may have felt upon dying that their loved ones were left unprotected, or their unfulfilled dreams were still attainable. Hauntings that occur at the missions may be the indelible emotional imprints of those who suffered the most, faced the greatest fears, or died with the dark feeling that they had failed to do all they could to make their lives worthy of admission to heaven.

The Mission San Buena Ventura, like all missions, has several ghosts. But the most notable spirit of this mission is more of a wanderer than other mission phantoms. For several decades, the old gray monk of Buena Ventura has been seen in downtown Ventura, crossing streets and wandering the sidewalks. At times, he sits on the banks of the Ventura River, admiring the view. He is seen on the mission ground, too, near a monument placed in remembrance of three padres buried in the church. Local ghost hunters believe the gray monk is one of those padres. Those who have seen him report a chill in the air as he approaches. Shock and fear disappear as the apparition smiles and extends his warm countenance.

THE HEADLESS BIKER

Camp Comfort
Highway 33, 1.5 miles south of Ojai
11969 Creek Road
Ojai 93231
(805) 654-3951

Camp Comfort County Park is nestled in a little valley 15 miles north of Ventura. The quiet campground gives the impression of a peaceful oasis not far from high-energy Los Angeles and the exciting Ventura-L.A. coastline. Tall trees and grassy meadows invite visitors to stay awhile and enjoy the quiet atmosphere, until the sunset. When darkness fills Camp Comfort, the atmosphere changes and eerie things begin to happen.

Camp Comfort is the permanent home of several spirits, and they tend to make the nights a little tense for some visitors. A big element in the park's mystique has to do with a vampire legend. It is said that in 1890 a vampire from Spain settled in the area. His attacks on local cattle and people led to a hunt for his sarcophagus. It was found near Creek Road guarded by a huge black dog. Upon opening the ornate stone casket, holy water from Mission Santa Barbara was sprinkled on the vampire's body as a few brave ranchers drove a stake through his heart. The black dog drove them off and for several months prevented others from investigating the fantastic reports of the vampire's death. Before long, the location of the sarcophagus was forgotten as weeds grew around it. But the huge black dog still guards the area, often passing through Camp Comfort. Several people have seen this dog on Creek Road as well. Its snarling, growling sounds echo off the hillsides as his feet pad along the blacktop.

Campers have also witnessed a lady in a wedding dress hitchhiking through the park. There is no information about her other than her general appearance. She is tall and slim with long light-brown hair. Her veil covers her face as she holds out her hand with her thumb pointing to the entrance of Camp Comfort.

The most often-sighted apparition in Camp Comfort is that of a motorcyclist. The easy rider passes through the park, allowing campers a chance to admire his classic Harley known as the "Indian," low and sleek with big tires and red fenders. Some witnesses hear that characteristic Harley rumble emanating from the big engine. This biker and his "hog" appear quite solid until he passes by and disappears into the darkness. The most startling thing about him is that he has no head. Psychic investigators believe the biker hit a low tree branch while riding through the mountains at high speed. Unaware of his death, he continues his night rides that include a slow cruise through Camp Comfort County Park.

THE GHOST OF CHAR-MAN

Creek Road Bridge
Creek Road between Highway 33 and the town of Ojai 93231

By day, the Ojai Valley is a bit of heaven. Orange groves cover the valley floor, growing around the quaint town of Ojai and nestling against the slopes of the surrounding hills. By night, things are a bit more unsettling and some of the sights along the roads coursing through the valley can make a traveler feel quite unwelcome. Tall oak trees seem to darken the night as they block out the moon and stars.

Two-lane Creek Road winds through the valley, connecting the main highway with Ojai. At night, a tired driver might have a little trouble with the curves if rain or fog obscure his vision. Local legend says that in the early 1950s, a man failed to make a curve near the intersection with Shelf Road, and his car ran off the road. His car burst into flames, burning him, but he was thrown from the wreckage. With his clothes on fire, he wandered into the brush, screaming for help. Perhaps he saw a distant light and thought it was a house or farm where he could find someone to call an ambulance. Whatever he thought, he never found the help he needed.

No one in the vicinity heard the sound of a wreck or the screams of the injured man. In the morning, the remains of the burned car were hauled away and officials searched the nearby brush and orchards. They found no body.

Within days, however, reports were called in to the police about an apparition on Creek Road Bridge, close to the site of the accident. At night, a wispy image of a man was seen. He staggered onto the road with charred clothing hanging from his arms and burned skin covering his face. Some people reported a terrible smell, no doubt the odor of burned flesh. The horrible apparition approaches both drivers and those on foot, waving his arms and trying to call out to them.

Other ghosts are seen on Creek Road. There are reports of a woman on horseback galloping on the road by moonlight. This ghost appears on the anniversary of the woman's death, caused when a snake spooked her horse. Another woman, wearing a wedding dress, is seen on the road in daylight. She was murdered nearby on her wedding day, it is supposed.

GHOST OF PETER LE BECK

Fort Tejon State Park
Grape Vine Canyon on Interstate 5
34 miles south of Bakersfield; P.O. Box 895
Lebec, 93243
(805) 248-6692

Peter Le Beck was one of a few trappers and hunters who dared enter the Mexican territory of California in the 1830s. Perhaps because he was French, the Mexicans viewed him with less suspicion than was cast upon Americans who attempted trade or business enterprises in the coastal settlements. Nothing is known of his personal history except the date of his death. It seems that a companion, or someone who knew Peter, buried him under an oak tree and marked the place with an inscription: "Peter Le Beck, killed by x bear, October 17, 1837." The harrowing death is enough to lead to a haunting, but 20 years later, Peter's rest was disturbed.

In 1854, the U.S. Army established a large fort at the Tejon site. Twenty buildings were constructed and filled with officers, troops, and their families. Some of the ladies noticed Le Beck's grave at the foot of the tall oak and persuaded the soldiers to relocate it to the fort's cemetery. It is not clear if Le Beck's bones were actually removed to the cemetery, for as soon as the digging starting, Peter's apparition appeared, and he has not yet returned to his rest. Some ghost hunters believe his remains were moved and that his apparition roams the grounds of Fort Tejon, searching for the new grave. This ghost is most often seen, however, near the oak tree. He wears buckskin clothing and black boots. Tucked in his belt is a large knife.

Many other ghosts roam Fort Tejon. Between 1854 and 1864, thousands of Indians were imprisoned here awaiting removal to lands not wanted by Yankee settlers. During imprisonment, hundreds died under the most miserable conditions. Buried in unmarked graves, they sometimes fill the old fort with cold spots and strange atmospheres.

One of the Indians held prisoner at the fort was Chief Black Bear. According to the historical records, he was hung from an oak tree that still stands about 300 yards from Le Beck's grave. The chief's ghost is often seen near the French trapper's grave, however. This has led to speculation that Chief Black Bear is the "x bear" referred to in the inscription on Le Beck's tree. Perhaps Peter was killed by the Indian chief who continued his renegade ways until he was hung by the soldiers 20 years later.

Psychic investigation by Richard Senate and others of the three remaining original buildings has revealed other hot spots for ghost hunts. At the orderlies' quarters, a phantom wagon appears inside the structure. Here, sensitive investigators have felt anger, frustration, and strong vibrations that generate impressions of a murder. The basement of the officer's quarters harbors a force investigators described as "terrifying," while on the upper floor, quiet conversations of women have been heard. A sense of sadness pervades the entire building reflecting the difficult, isolated life at Fort Tejon. The mess hall, behind the reconstructed barracks, replays the sounds of noisy conversations of hungry soldiers.

MUGU ROCK GHOST OF PRINCESS HUENEME

Point Mugu
Highway 1 (Pacific Coast Highway near Oxnard)

Point Mugu's unmistakable landmark is a huge rock formed when construction crews cut a roadbed through a ridge of the Santa Monica range. As you approach the point from north or south, the rock stands stark, separating Highway 1 from the Pacific Ocean. Just offshore sits another, much smaller rock. This rock is a natural part of the coastal terrain and, many believe, the remnant of a Chumash Indian legend. It is awash by the surf that sometimes reveals the image of Princess Hueneme and her husband.

The legend tells of a beautiful Indian princess who won the heart of a brave man, one of hundreds who sought her hand in marriage. They started married life with happiness and love that was the talk of tribes in the region. But it wasn't long before a wicked woman entered the village and destroyed this blissful marriage. Practicing black magic, the woman attracted the attention of Hueneme's husband and led him away. After days of misery, Hueneme mustered her courage and went after them. She succeeded in breaking the witch's hold on her husband, but after returning to their village, their lives were never the same. Curses and spells kept them from rekindling their love and promised to cast shadows upon them forever. Despondent, the princess waded into the ocean, allowing the surf and riptides to end her life. Her husband raced to the site only to see her disappear beneath the waves. Raging with grief, he jumped into the sea, hoping to die with Hueneme.

The Chumash believe the gods granted their wish to always be together by turning them both to stone. At this point, modern ghost hunters backtrack a bit, then focus on the possibility of a double suicide at a site perfect for the act. Rough surf and intersecting currents make the water around Point Mugu dangerous, even for surfers and well-equipped SCUBA divers. Psychic study of this spot has discovered images of a blue scarf waving in the breeze over the rock revered by the Chumash as Princess Hueneme. Others have reported seeing Hueneme sitting on the rock with surf foaming around her feet.

A man who crashed his car into the massive rock in August 1994 made a modern contribution to the haunted atmosphere of Point Mugu. Accusations of child molestation were too much for the 65-year-old man. A quiet drive along the coast seemed like a good idea, but it failed to rid his mind of worry and shame. Approaching Point Mugu rock from the south, the stony prominence stood straight ahead, cold and hard, as if inviting an end to his miseries. He hit the rock at high speed, freeing his spirit of earthly problems in an instant. The emotional imprint at the site on the south side of the rock is strong. It is experienced as the sound of tires leaving the asphalt and racing over gravel and dirt. Some psychic investigators sense a crash, then great sorrow.

GHOST GUESTS

The Mission Inn
3649 Mission Inn Avenue
Riverside 92501
(951) 822-5425
www.missioninn.com

The Mission Inn is, as its name suggests, a replica of California's missions designed as an inn for weary travelers. That's the role played by the old Spanish missions. The Mission Inn, though, was opened in 1876 without the strict Jesuit rules, forced labor, meager meals, and miserable sleeping quarters. Instead, the original Mission Inn offered safe, clean, comfortable rooms and a restaurant that served exceptional food. The place was expanded and upgraded between 1903 and 1933, then underwent a major eight-year renovation, reopening in 1993 as the focal point of Riverside's downtown. Throughout the extensive construction and remodeling, some guests found that they couldn't tear themselves away from the comfortable inn. The reason may be that they are dead and have nowhere else to go.

Inn and restaurant staff members often glimpse these non-paying guests. Sometimes large groups are seen at the fireplace in the lobby. These apparitions appear to carry on animated conversations but vanish if a living person tries to join in. The ghosts are dressed in clothing from the late 1800s, with the men sporting mustaches while the graceful women move about in long gowns. Another group of Victorian-era guests has been seen in the lobby by the stairs.

Some of the hotel's ghosts know how to have a good time. Loud parties have been reported to the management, who found only an empty room. Poolside, the sound of exotic birds has been heard. No animals are kept at the inn these days, but from 1876 to about 1900, the original owner, Frank Miller, housed several birds in cages to give the pool area an exotic atmosphere.

Waiters in the restaurant often see couples or foursomes walk in and seat themselves. The odd thing is that these guests are dressed in elegant Victorian or Edwardian attire and they vanish before ordering a meal. Sometimes, invisible guests lift glasses from trays, move dishes around, or disturb place settings.

SARAH AND DAVID, UNITED IN DEATH

Morey Mansion Inn
190 Terracina Boulevard
Redlands 92375
(909) 336-6657
www.moreymansion.com/

Sarah and David Morey came to California ahead of the crowd. They arrived about 1880 when there was plenty of land available, few government regulations, and not much to impede the pursuit of their dreams. Sarah and David dreamed of owning their own business, something that would provide an essential, basic product to an industry with an unlimited future. Somehow they came up with the idea of a nursery for orange tree seedlings. With Southern California's climate and soil, this proved to be a fantastic business. In just a few short years, the Moreys were rich and busy building their mansion.

Right away, the Morey mansion became the gem of the community. It was lavish in its furnishings and blended several architectural styles.

Sarah and David enjoyed nearly 20 years in this spectacular home.

Sarah departed first. She died in 1901. Lonely and despondent, David decided he couldn't stay in the house. He thought San Diego might be nice, for he could run his business from any city in Southern California. A buyer for the mansion was found and papers were signed. But giving up their beloved home didn't seem right to David. Looking around, he no doubt felt Sarah's presence as he recalled their happy years in the mansion. She was still there, and he couldn't leave. So, David walked upstairs, wrote a short note saying he could not live without Sarah, and blew his brains out.

Several séances and psychic investigations have demonstrated that the loving couple still reside in the Morey mansion. They appear as cold spots, create the sound of footsteps on the stairs or second-floor hallway, move doors, and cause the lights to flicker. In the tower room, the sound of pacing footsteps is heard. No one is seen in the room, but a sudden cold breeze may strike the inquisitive person brave enough to open the door and take a look. Sometimes, the Moreys are seen as a nearly full apparition together with a girl and a thin, elderly man dressed as a servant. All are dressed in late-19th-century clothing and appear to be quite happy.

A 1999 Home and Garden TV special on haunted houses featured the Morey Mansion Inn. Investigators for the program believe the inn had more ghosts than guests in its four guestrooms.

GHOST OF YOUNG MAGDALENA

Mission San Juan Capistrano
26801 Ortega Highway
San Juan Capistrano 92675
(949) 234-1300
www.missionsjc.com/

Mission San Juan Capistrano is the fabled home of the swallows that return each year from Argentina on Saint Joseph's Day, March 19. Their annual appearance adds to the allure of what was known as the jewel of the missions. Surrounded by beautiful gardens and adobe walls, the old stone church and some of the newer reconstructed elements block out the modern world, offering an 18th-century tranquility for visitors, and a refuge for ghosts.

Mission San Juan Capistrano was founded on October 30, 1775, but an Indian uprising drove the Spanish padres away for a year. A second ceremony was held November 1, 1776, making this mission the seventh in the California chain. The first church on this site was nothing more than a hut made of mud. It was replaced by an adobe church in 1778 and enlarged to become the mission's chapel in 1785. The great stone church, completed in 1806, was built by using quarried limestone to cement rocks into seven-foot-thick walls. As the mission community grew, dormitories, shops, kitchens, a library, and other buildings were added, forming a long colonnade. Inner and outer courtyards were formed to enclose gardens that still flourish today.

In 1812, the rules of the mission fathers were strict and punishment of a trespasser was swift and painful. A young girl, Magdalena, knew the rules, but she could not set aside her desires for a certain young man whose identity remains unknown. Speculation is that he was a monk or priest in training. They met in hidden places, sharing forbidden moments of romance. With so many Indians, Spanish soldiers, and priests moving about the mission, it was only a matter of time before their indiscretion was uncovered.

Magdalena's penance was long and difficult, starting with carrying a candle around the mission courtyard, lighting all the dark places, from sunrise to sunset without rest. On October 8, 1812, she rose before dawn, dressed in warm clothing, and lit a candle. She had completed less than an hour of this penance when a major earthquake stopped her. Magdalena stood frozen in fear as the walls of the great mission shook and cracked, then fell, crushing her and 39 others to death. Magdalena's ghost is still doing penance, however. Her apparition is seen, lit by candlelight, near the reconstructed stone walls of the great church, the site of her death.

A faceless man dressed in a brown robe haunts the inner courtyard. He moves about as though he is searching for something or someone. He appears to be a monk. Ghost hunters speculate that he was Magdalena's lover.

Several other ghosts and ghostly phenomena have been reported at the mission. The apparition of a woman concealed by a black or brown shawl has been seen standing under an arch at the north corner of the inner courtyard. A headless soldier on horseback passes through the outer courtyard, most often from north to south. In the bell tower, invisible spirits pull the ropes, sounding the mission's bells at dawn and again at midafternoon.

GHOSTS OF THE WHALEY HOUSE

2476 San Diego Avenue
San Diego 92110
(619) 297-7511
www.whaleyhouse.org/

The restored Whaley House of San Diego's Old Town sits resplendent in the sun, its beautiful red bricks, white wooden balconies and window frames, and trim landscaping hide the fact that it is nearly 150 years old. Inside, the modern world slips away quickly. Antiques and the charming historic atmosphere make it easy to get a palpable sense of life in the 1850s. The ghosts may have something to do with that too. They move about, mostly unseen, making it clear that they are still here and the house is still their home.

There is little doubt of that. After all, the U.S. Department of Commerce and the State of California designated this place a "haunted house." Several spirit and psychic investigations have documented the presence of at least seven ghosts. These include Thomas and Anna Eloise Whaley, their dog Dolly, a little girl named Carrie Washburn, a young Native American woman who worked in the house as a servant, a workman or handyman, and a rogue named Yankee Jim Robinson.

The presence of Yankee Jim's ghost makes the Whaley House a good example of a haunting that occurs in a structure erected after the death of a person. It turns out that the Whaley House was constructed on the site of the Old Town gallows. It is estimated that five to 10 men were hung on that gallows. One of those unfortunate fellows was Yankee Jim Robinson, hung in 1852 for stealing the town's pilot boat. His execution was gruesome because the rope failed to

San Diego's Whaley House has been called one of the most haunted houses in America. (Photo by T. W. Storer.)

snap his neck. As a result, he struggled for 15 minutes, until the spirit left his body and ended his misery.

In 1856 the old gallows was dismantled, the land cleared, and Thomas Whaley constructed his two-story brick house. The archway separating the music room from the parlor was placed on the site of the gallows from which Yankee Jim suffered such an agonizing death. Today, under the archway sensitive visitors feel a cold spot and tightness about the neck as if the gallows rope has been placed for their execution. Some have reported seeing the wispy image of a man hanging from the archway, while others have heard disembodied footsteps at this location and on the second floor. Since as many as 10 men were hung on this spot, it is possible that one or more ghosts are present here. Some believe the ghost of Juan Verdugo, hung in 1853, haunts the home.

In the kitchen, ghost hunters and tourists have seen a blond girl named Carrie Washburn. Ten-year-old Carrie lived nearby and often played in the Whaley yard, occasionally dashing into the kitchen to get cookies with other neighborhood children. One day in the 1860s she ran across the yard and was caught about the neck by a clothesline. Her trachea was damaged, making it impossible for her to breathe. She was carried into the Whaleys' kitchen and placed on the table, where she died. Carrie apparently loved to visit the Whaleys, because she still dashes across the yard into the kitchen.

The ghost of the workman is seldom seen in the house, but he has been spotted in the yard. His apparition appears as a vertical cloud of gray smoke about six feet tall. He glides across the yard toward the house but disappears before reaching the back door.

A female Native American servant has been seen in the large room that served as the San Diego County courthouse and records repository in the 1860s. After the courthouse was moved, the woman set up a small living quarters in the northwest corner of the room. At this spot, in August 1992, a photographer captured her ghost on film. The photograph is on display in the Whaley House, together with several other ghost photos taken by amateur and professional photographers.

The ghost of Anna Eloise Whaley can be found in many of the photographs on display in her home. She has been seen sitting in a rocking chair on the second floor, making it move, and standing near the window in the same room. Investigators believe Mrs. Whaley sits in the chair rocking her infant son, Thomas Whaley, Jr., who died in this room. Sometimes, the sounds of an infant crying are heard here.

Anna Whaley also appears on the ground floor of the house. In 1997, a group of 11 people saw her apparition leave the dining room, walk down the corridor, and enter the kitchen. Her partial apparition, dressed in a long gown, has been seen often in the music room. Docents reported the sound of piano music coming from the room at times when the house is closed to visitors. At various locations within the house, the fragrance of lavender perfume has been detected.

Anna Whaley may be present on the staircase too. This haunting arises from a dispute that arose in 1871 concerning the continued operation of the courthouse in the Whaley building. Thomas Whaley demanded the county honor its lease for the space, while certain county officials tried to relocate the facility to a site in the newer part of San Diego. The dispute escalated, polarizing the neighborhood, and then became an armed confrontation. When tempers cooled and a more calm atmosphere prevailed, Thomas slipped away to take care of urgent business in San Francisco. While he was away, a group of armed men entered his home, held his family at gunpoint on the staircase, and removed all courthouse furniture and implements as well as stacks of county records. Anna and the children were terrorized. An imprint from this experience remains on the stairs. Paranormal investigations have identified a cold spot on the ninth step, believed to the place Anna and her children held each other under the threatening gaze of armed men.

When Thomas returned from San Francisco, he was furious to learn of this violation of his home and the threat to his family. He sought financial restitution and social redemption, but county officials refused to acknowledge that the incident took place. Thomas's ghost, seen as a lifelike apparition in many parts of the house, still keeps a watchful eye for intruders. Historians and ghost hunters believe he never forgave the men who broke into his house and threatened his family. Even after his death, he remains in the house, guarding against another violation of his beloved home.

KATE MORGAN AND THE GHOSTS OF THE GRAND OLD HOTEL

Hotel del Coronado
1500 Orange Avenue
Coronado 92118
(619) 435-6611
www.hoteldel.com

Kate Morgan arrived in San Diego from her home in Visalia, California, anxious and depressed, no doubt wondering if she was doing the right thing. She had received a letter from her estranged husband, Tom, asking her to meet him at the Hotel del Coronado.

The magnificent Hotel del Coronado is still home to the 1890s murder victim Kate Morgan. (Photo by T. W. Storer.)

When she arrived and saw the opulent hotel by the sea, she might have thought that Tom's gambling had paid off and they would be reunited. Still, she waited three days without seeing him. Guests of the hotel noticed her. Later when questioned about Kate, they said she was tense, morose, and, at times, appeared ill. There was speculation of stomach cancer but some evidence suggests that she consulted a San Diego physician about the possibility of pregnancy. During these three days, Kate wandered about the beautiful hotel. She did nothing unusual except purchase a handgun at a local shop. There is no record of Tom Morgan checking into the hotel, but we know when Kate Morgan checked out. On Thanksgiving morning, 1892, she was found dead at the foot of the stairs leading to the beach.

The police investigation concluded it was suicide. But there is considerable evidence that she was murdered, perhaps by her husband, Tom. Some stories that have taken on an air of fact hold that Kate found Tom at the Hotel del Coronado carousing with another woman. Despondent, she committed suicide with the gun she had purchased. The problem with this story is that Kate was killed with a .44-caliber bullet. Her gun was a .32 caliber. Also, Kate's body was in a position not consistent with suicide.

Whether Kate Morgan died from suicide or murder, her death was the tragic culmination of a troubled life complicated by a bad marriage and possibly a pregnancy. This is the stuff that leads to hauntings. Indeed, the Hotel del Coronado is considered by many ghost hunters to be one of the most haunted hotels in America.

Not long after Kate's death, light poltergeist activity started in room 3502 (numbered 502 in 1892). Spectral clouds were seen in this room. Lights turned on and off, objects were moved, and cold spots and a profound sense of sadness have been detected. However, Kate did not stay in this room. In 1892, room 502 was occupied by a maid who had befriended Kate during her short stay. Even more curious, the maid disappeared one day after Kate's funeral. Some investigators suggest that she, too, was murdered. Whatever her fate, paranormal activity in her former room was at one time so frightening that 3502 was locked up and made off-limits to staff and guests.

In Kate's former room, 3312 (numbered 302 in 1892), apparitions have been seen by guests, cold spots identified, and soft moaning heard in the middle of the night. A woman dressed in a black lace gown has been reported floating around the room. Sometimes she wanders the corridors and descends the stairs to the beach before fading away.

Psychic investigations of other parts of the magnificent resort concluded that there are several spiritual entities residing here. Some of them gather for loud parties behind locked doors in rooms that have no living guests. Pale or semisolid apparitions have been seen on the main stairs, in the bar, and around the swimming pool.

In 1975, a story circulated around the hotel that a woman's body was found buried under several feet of sand when the swimming pool was constructed. Perhaps this was the body of Kate Morgan's friend who disappeared only days after poor Kate's death.

GHOST OF THE SUICIDE SERVANT

Villa Montezuma
1925 K Street
San Diego 92102
(619) 239-2211

The Villa Montezuma is an architectural gem. A blend of the Victorian style with some older English elements, it features intricate patterns in wood that flow around arched windows, paneled segments, and the cupola. This beautiful house was built in 1887 by opera singer Jesse Shepard. Reminiscent of the much larger Winchester Mystery House in San Jose, California, Villa Montezuma was also built for spiritual practices. Today, it is a museum operated by the San Diego Historical Society.

Jesse Shepard achieved fame as an opera singer, but he was best known as a spiritualist or occultist. He built a special room in his grand house—just as Sarah Winchester did—and conducted séances. Using his magnificent singing voice, he summoned spirits of the dead. This practice damaged his popularity among the higher social

The ghost of opera singer Jesse Shepard and his suicidal servant have been spotted in Shepard's Victorian Villa Montezuma. (Photo by T. W. Storer.)

circles in San Diego, so Jesse moved to Europe, where he died. But that didn't stop him from returning to his beloved home in Southern California. Many staff members of the museum, as well as visitors, sense his presence in the séance room. Ice-cold spots can be detected together with a feeling that an invisible person is standing close by.

The image of a sad face has also been reported in a window of the cupola. This may be an apparition of Jesse Shepard, but some people think it is the ghost of a servant who hung himself in the room. Historical records indicate that the servant's wife had died. Despondent, her dedicated husband joined her through a reliable technique, hanging. The ghost of the servant's wife is also believed to roam Villa Montezuma. Ghost hunters have seen misty images of an older woman.

GHOST OF THE YOUNG SAILOR

Star of India
Maritime Museum of San Diego
1492 North Harbor Avenue
San Diego 92101
(619) 234-9153
www.sdmaritime.com

All ships are haunted. In particular are those that have remained afloat for over a hundred years, rounded the treacherous Cape Horn, and sailed the great oceans. The sweep of the hull, rake of tall masts, and solid feel of timeworn decks evoke a romantic notion that the great ship is, indeed, a timeless thing of beauty and great strength upon which much love was lavished. So it is with the *Star of India,* berthed at San Diego's floating Maritime Museum. She stands proud as the oldest active sailing ship in the world. Several other vessels join the *Star of India* at the museum.

Launched in 1863, she sailed for 35 years as the British flag vessel *Euterpe.* She carried cargo of all kinds plus emigrants between England, India, Australia, Hawaii, and ports in South America. Those years were prosperous for her owners and officers, but the inevitable tragedies of sea duty did occur. Passengers and crew died on board. There were accidents and collisions with other ships, and even a mutiny. She sailed through storms that threatened to sink her, skirted huge icebergs, and sat becalmed under a blazing sun in the South Pacific with her water supply putrid from the heat.

In 1898, the *Euterpe* was sold to an American shipping company and renamed the *Star of India.* Refitted, she carried salmon from fisheries in Alaska to West Coast ports. By 1923, the iron-hulled sailing vessel was truly an anachronism among modern steam-powered ships. She was left in an Oakland, California, estuary to rot. In 1927, the *Star* was rescued by a group of sailing buffs and others interested in maritime history. But it wasn't until 1976 that she was restored to her former glory as an active sailing vessel with a skilled crew and opened as a museum at San Diego's waterfront.

Through all of this, the ghosts of the *Star of India* remained aboard. In fact, during her stay at the Oakland estuary, a caretaker saw the ghost of a young man many times. It is believed that the apparition was that of a young and inexperienced sailor named John Campbell. The unfortunate John Campbell started his first and only voyage as a stowaway aboard the *Euterpe*. Only days after leaving Glasgow, he and two others were discovered hiding in a locker. Turning back to port was unthinkable, so John and his mates were put to work as seamen. After a miserable life in abject poverty, John Campbell found himself on board a beautiful ship, en route to New Zealand, with lively mates, a warm bunk, and three meals per day. His life seemed to be taking a great turn for the better until the day he was sent aloft to work the high yards of the mainmast. The view from up there was breathtaking but the work was treacherous. Pausing with exhilaration, John waved to a friend and lost his hold on the ropes. He fell 125 feet to the deck, breaking his legs in several places. He died three days later. His body was committed to the sea but his spirit has remained on board his ship.

The apparitions of the young sailor that were so common in the 1920s are less frequent these days. But sensitive ghost hunters still perceive a touch on the shoulder by an invisible being. Cold spots are also detected near the mainmast at the place where John hit the deck. The sound of creaking wood and billowing sails can also be heard when the decks are quiet and ghost hunters succeed in blocking out the modern world.

Paranormal activity described as "gentle" has been reported at a number of places on the ship. Some of this has occurred in the anchor chain locker in the bow. Here, hundreds of feet of heavy chain were stored and paid out when the anchor was weighed. During a cruise to Alaska, a Chinese crewman was caught by the chain. It flew across the locker, through the cat's eye (a hole in the hull), lowering the anchor into the sea. This sudden, horrible death left a strong imprint in the chain locker. Visitors experience an icy cold spot on the right side of the room together with a creepy feeling that some unseen person is standing close by. One ghost hunter picked up the sound of an anchor chain rubbing on the deck.

A nighttime tour of the *Star of India* offered by the museum staff is a chilling way to explore this magnificent ship.

Another haunted vessel at the Maritime Museum of San Diego is the ferryboat *Berkeley*. The ornate, Victorian-age ferryboat shuttled terrified passengers across San Francisco Bay in the hours after the great earthquake of 1906. This fine example of 19th-century ferryboats has a ghost. The apparition of a man wearing a fedora has been seen on the port (left) side of the ship walking the deck. He could be the ghost of John O. Norbom, who was killed in an explosion in the men's restroom on the main deck on January 13, 1911. Any one of several others who died on the *Berkeley* could be the fedora-clad ghost. Another possibility is that the apparition reported was a haunting, or emotional imprint of a passenger who loved his daily trips across San Francisco between work and home.

GHOST OF ROGER WHITAKER

Horton Grand Hotel
311 Island Avenue
San Diego 92101
(619) 544-1886
www.hortongrand.com

The Horton Grand Hotel is a good example of a modern building haunted by the spirit of a man who died in a preceding structure on the site. Ghost hunters should always consider this as the basis of a haunting when the history of a building or recent history of the location don't give up clues that contribute to an understanding of reported paranormal phenomena.

Room 309 of the Horton Grand Hotel contains a diary in which guests have recorded their experiences. Entries include lamp pulls that sway for 30 minutes or more, violent motions of the bed and lamp, mysterious movement of curtains and the mirror above the TV, heavy footsteps, the impression of a man's body on the bed cover, hands of poker dealt from a deck left stacked by the room's occupants, lights going off and on, and numerous other ghostly tricks.

Guests in room 309 have felt the presence of a man and the disembodied touch of a cold hand on the shoulder. Some have been pushed around a little as if the ghost were trying to get them to move to another part of the room. At times, the ghost responsible for these experiences has been seen. He has appeared quite solid, to the extent that a woman once asked him for directions then watched him disappear. This ghost is dressed in clothing from the mid-19th century, possibility that of a rancher or horseman.

Based on the variety of reports from ghost hunters and hotel guests, it seems likely that several ghosts haunt the Horton Grand Hotel. Indeed, more than one witness has reported seeing groups of people in period clothing. Psychic Shelly Deegan saw 20 ghosts dressed in Victorian clothing ascend the stairs to the third floor. Two ghosts named Gus and Henry were also identified by psychic investigators.

But the best known ghost at the Horton Grand is Roger Whitaker. Roger was a rogue and a gambler. As such, several stories are told about the way he died. Some believe Roger was a pimp who operated out of several brothels but could not pay off his huge gambling debts. To make matters worse, Roger was caught cheating at cards. He dashed from the poker table and managed to elude several men chasing after him. Making his way to his hotel room, he hid in an armoire. Someone gave him away and the raucous mob burst through his door and fired several shots into the armoire, killing Roger. His body was dumped into a swamp at the back of the hotel. Years later, in 1886, the ramshackle hotel was torn down and the Grand Hotel constructed on the site.

Another story describes Roger as a man engaged to be married who could not give up his habit of gambling and visiting local brothels. His future father-in-law learned of Roger's recreational habits and could not bear the thought of his daughter marrying such a man. So, one night in 1843, the man made certain no wedding would take place. As Roger entered his hotel, shots rang out, killing the would-be groom.

Today's Horton Grand Hotel was constructed in 1986 from several elements salvaged from the two hotels built on the site in 1886: the Grand and the Kahle Saddlery. In spite of these changes, Roger Whitaker still haunts the location of his death. He might be confused with the architectural differences, but he seems to like the new hotel and its modern amenities.

The room above Roger's may be haunted too. Guests in room 309 have been kept awake all night by creaking sounds that seem to be coming from the ceiling as if a group of people in room 409 are dancing.

GHOSTS OF THE OLD FOLKS

El Campo Santo Cemetery
2400 San Diego Avenue
San Diego 92110

This 1849 vintage Roman Catholic cemetery is the final resting place for about 500 people. Most of the departed seem to be resting in peace, but there are quite a few who are unhappy. And they aren't shy about expressing their dissatisfaction.

For 40 years, El Campo Santo was a well-kept, peaceful cemetery with graves that were visited and decorated by family and friends who lived nearby. By 1889, however, the population center of San Diego shifted from Old Town to New Town, some distance away, and fewer people were left to care for the graves. As a result, El Campo Santo became one of those neglected cemeteries with fading grave markers, decaying fences, and weed-covered plots. Thinking that no one would care, the City of San Diego cleared a path through the cemetery for a horse-drawn streetcar line. Several headstones were destroyed and graves covered by the right-of-way. By 1942 the dirt passageway was widened, paved, and named San Diego Avenue. Interested citizens, including those who claimed to have relatives buried in the cemetery, complained about these developments, but for many years, the city officials gave it little consideration. Then, in the early 1990s, ground-piercing radar located 18 graves under the street. These were marked with white-painted crosses that appear to some motorists as parking space markers.

Beginning in 1889, the desecration of these graves has created several hauntings in El Campo Santo and nearby buildings. Ghost hunters have reported disembodied voices, many chilling cold spots, and apparitions of Native Americans, Hispanic pioneers, and criminals such as Yankee Jim Robinson.

Jim Robinson left the gold diggings of the northern Sierra in 1851

El Campo Santo cemetery in the final resting place for more than 500 people. Some of them wander about the neighborhood creating poltergeist activity. (Photo by T. W. Storer.)

for the sunny hills of San Diego. It is suspected that he left a lynch mob in his dust, hoping to blend in with the Yankees who were swelling the population of the former sleepy little town. But Jim was a troublemaker. In 1852 he was arrested for stealing a boat owned by the harbor authority. Jim resisted his arrest, claiming he was just borrowing the boat for a short while. In the melee, he was struck in the head, leaving him sick and delirious throughout his brief trial. Not yet recovered from his injury, Yankee Jim was hung. But this was a heinous execution, for the rope failed to break his neck. Instead of a quick death, Jim strangled in the noose for 15 minutes before he gave up the ghost. Today, his grave in El Campo Santo is a starting point used by many ghost hunters. Jim's ghost is believed to haunt the nearby Whaley House as well as the shady little graveyard.

The ghost of Native American Antonio Garra is often seen in El

Campo Santo. Chief of the local Cupeno tribe, Garra fought for the rights of his people by leading a rebellion against the city in 1850. The townspeople were sufficiently terrorized that they tried Garra and handed him a death sentence. In another heinous execution, the chief was marched into El Campo Santo, ordered to stand by a freshly dug grave, and then killed by a firing squad. Today, the ghost of Chief Antonio Garra is described by ghost hunters as a "spectral gentleman" wearing the clothing of a Mexican cowboy. He is seen gliding a foot or two above the ground near his grave.

An unidentified woman in a long dress typical of the mid-19th century has also been seen moving along the south wall of the cemetery. She appears to be solid and easy to mistake for a living person, until she disappears at the end of the walk.

On the street in front of El Campo Santo, car alarms are often triggered in vehicles parked over graves. Misty figures of people in period costumes are commonly seen gliding over the sidewalk of San Diego Avenue in front of the cemetery. Nearby businesses report paranormal events described as poltergeist activity. Perhaps the ghosts of El Campos Santo, whose earthly remains are covered by the pavement of San Diego Avenue, believe that the street belongs to them.

CASINO GHOSTS

The Casino
1 Casino Way
Avalon, Catalina Island 91304
(310) 510-0179
www.santacatalinaislandco.com

Catalina Island rises out of the sea like a jewel, shining under the Southern California sun. On clear days details of the island can be seen from the mainland, beckoning people with adventurous souls to hop on the ferry or the seaplane and travel 26 miles to this island paradise.

As you approach from the sea, the first and most impressive landmark that comes into view is the towering Casino, standing at the north end of Avalon Bay. The round, 12-story structure was built in the 1920s, opening with a spectacular ceremony on May 29, 1929.

The Casino at Avalon on Santa Catalina Island stands as a beacon to visitors who make the 26-mile voyage from the mainland.

The white walls and red tile roof blend with the Mediterranean architecture of many buildings in Avalon and create the impression of a very distant place and time.

The domed-ceiling theatre, art gallery, museum, and ballroom offer fascinating glimpses into another era. In the 1930s and 1940s, every major big band in America performed in the Casino ballroom with live broadcasts over the CBS radio network. In those days, Catalina and its fabulous ballroom were a world apart from the stress of the Depression and World War II. People went there to relax, forget their troubles, and enjoy the best life had to offer. Some liked it so much that death could not take them away.

In the 1930s, a woman was murdered in the women's restroom on the mezzanine. Her spirit remains, creating ice-cold spots and a creepy feeling that someone is watching while personal business is conducted. Nearby poltergeist activity has been attributed to the ghost of the murder victim.

Several ghosts who manifest by cold spots, footsteps, and even organ music haunt the bar adjacent to the ballroom. These ghosts are believed to be gangsters who were killed in or around the Casino. Some of them speak in soft tones, whispering cryptic messages.

The ghost of William Wrigley, the chewing-gum magnate and builder of the Casino, has been heard and seen in the lobby. He creates crashing sounds as if he is displeased with the placement of chairs and wall lights. Sometimes, Bill Wrigley drops into the theatre to watch a movie. He is quiet, but movie watchers get that creepy feeling that there is someone in the empty seat in the row behind them who is watching them.

GHOST OF THE WESTERN WRITER

Zane Grey Hotel
19 Chimes Tower Road, P.O. Box 216
Avalon, Catalina Island 91304
(310) 510-0966

Zane Grey (1872-1939) wrote 89 books in his lifetime, bringing the excitement and romance of the Old West to millions of readers.

But rather than settle down on a ranch in Texas or New Mexico, this Ohio native built his home on Santa Catalina Island. Here, he found rugged beauty, a relaxing sense of adventure, and an opportunity to pursue the great loves of his life. In 1926, after building his Indian pueblo-style home on a ridge overlooking Avalon, he explained why he chose that particular site: "I used to climb that mountain trail that overlooked the Pacific and here a thousand times I shut my eyes and gave myself over to sensorial perceptions. . . . It is an environment that means enchantment to me. Sea and mountain! Breeze and roar of surf! Music of birds! Solitude and tranquillity! A place for rest, dream, peace, sleep. I could write here and be at peace."

In his sprawling two-story house, Zane Grey wrote some of his best westerns, but he also wrote about baseball and sport fishing. He gathered a huge array of fishing equipment, baseball souvenirs, a substantial library, and a collection of western-style furniture. It is no wonder that Zane stayed on after his death, unable to leave his beloved home, filled with the riches of his life, perched on the ridge above Avalon Bay.

There is no doubt, Zane Grey is still in residence and not too displeased that his home is now a hotel. He is seen as a shadowy figure stepping into the hallway from his wife's former bedroom, now named the Purple Sage room after one of his books. He walks the corridor to his favorite rooms: the living room where he kept some of his fishing gear, the Stairs of Sand, the Drift Fence rooms (currently the manager's suite), and the Desert Gold room, Zane's former study.

If his misty image is not seen, Zane is often heard. Footsteps sound in the hallways, on the stairs, and around the swimming pool. Cold spots sometimes laced with the odors of tobacco also mark his passage. Those who have witnessed paranormal activity generated by Zane Grey feel that he is not trying to disturb guests of the hotel or keep staff from their work. Zane appears without creating a sense of uneasiness. He is just looking over his beloved pueblo, quite pleased that visitors love the place too.

If you travel to Santa Catalina Island, check out these other haunted places.

Banning House Lodge, located at Two Harbors, 22 miles from

Avalon, (310) 510-2800. Look for the ghost of a bearded, older man dressed in a long coat and hat.

Clubhouse Bar and Grill, 100 Country Club Road, Avalon 90704, (310) 510-7404. A ghost dressed in a 1930s Chicago Cubs baseball uniform haunts the bar.

Glenmore Plaza Hotel, 120 Summer Avenue, Avalon 90704, (310) 510-0017. Several witnesses have seen a comedian ghost.

Hotel Catalina, 126 Whitney Avenue, Avalon 90704, (310) 510-0184. A ghost rearranges furniture, keeps things clean and neat, and turns off lights.

Sighting Report Form

Photocopy and enlarge the form on the next page to a standard 8.5 x 11 inch format. This form should be completed right after a sighting. If the ghost hunt is performed by a group, a designated leader should assume the role of reporter. The reporter is responsible for completing this form.

The reporter and each witness should make a statement, either audio or written, describing in full their experience at the site. Date, sign, and label these statements with a reference number identical to the REPORT # on the sighting report form. Attach the statements to the Report Form.

SIGHTING REPORT

SITE NAME _____ REPORT # _____
LOCATION _____ DATE: _____
_____ TIME: _____
REPORTER _____ SITE # _____
WITNESSES _____
_____
_____

DESCRIPTION OF APPARITION
_____
_____

temperature change   [] YES   [] NO
auditory phenomena   [] YES   [] NO
telekinesis   [] YES   [] NO
visual phenomena   [] YES   [] NO
other phenomena   [] YES   [] NO
Description: _____

Use the reverse side for diagrams, maps, and drawings.

SPECIFIC LOCATION WITHIN SITE: _____

PREVIOUS SIGHTINGS AT THIS SITE?
                           [] YES   [] NO
Reference:
_____

Summary:
_____
_____

RECORDS:
audio   [] YES   [] NO   Ref. No. _____
video   [] YES   [] NO   Ref. No. _____
photo   [] YES   [] NO   Ref. No. _____
Summary of Records:
_____

Disposition of Records:
_____

WITNESS STATEMENTS (Summary): _____
_____
_____

audio   [] YES   [] NO
written   [] YES   [] NO
Disposition of statements: _____
_____
_____

Suggested Reading

BOOKS

Anderson, Jean. *The Haunting of America: Ghost Stories from Our Past.* Boston: Houghton-Mifflin, 1973.

Auerbach, Loyd. *ESP, Hauntings and Poltergeists: A Parapsychologist's Handbook.* New York: Warner Books, 1986.

———. *Ghost Hunting: How to Investigate the Paranormal.* Oakland, Calif.: Ronin Publishing, 2004.

Baker, Robert A, and Joe Nickell. *Missing Pieces: How to Investigate Ghosts, UFOs, Psychics, & Other Mysteries.* Buffalo, N.Y.: Prometheus Books, 1992.

Bardens, Dennis. *Ghosts and Hauntings.* IUniverse, 2000.

Bayless, Raymond. *Apparitions and Survival After Death.* New Hyde Park, N.Y.: University Books, 1973.

Beckett, John. *World's Weirdest True Ghost Stories.* New York: Sterling Publishing, 1992.

Bradley, Nancy, and Vincent Gaddis. *Gold Rush Ghosts.* Garberville, Calif.: Borderland Sciences Research Foundation, Inc. 1990.

Browne, Sylvia. *Adventures of a Psychic.* New York: Penguin Books, 1990.

Burnett, Claudine. *Haunted Long Beach.* Long Beach, Calif.: Historical Society of Long Beach, 1996.

Cohen, Daniel. *The Encyclopedia of Ghosts.* New York: Dodd, Mead, 1984.

Cornell, Tony. *Investigating the Paranormal.* New York: Helix Press, 2002.

Dennett, Preston E. *California Ghosts: True Accounts of Hauntings in the Golden State*. Atglen, Penn.: Schiffer Publishing, 2004.

Dwyer, Jeff. *Ghost Hunter's Guide to the San Francisco Bay Area*. Gretna, La.: Pelican Publishing, 2005.

Ebon, Martin, ed. *The Signet Handbook of Parapsychology*. New York: New American Library, 1978.

Editors of Time-Life Books. *Hauntings*. Alexandria, Vir.: Time-Life Books, 1991.

——. *Phantom Encounters*. Alexandria, Vir.: Time-Life Books, 1991.

Finucane, R. C. *Appearances of the Dead: A Cultural History of Ghosts*. Buffalo, N.Y.: Prometheus Books, 1984.

Holzer, Hans. *America's Haunted Houses*. Stanford, Conn.: Longmeadow Press, 1991.

——. *Real Hauntings*. New York: Barnes and Noble, 1995.

Jacobsen, Laurie, and Marc Wanamaker. *Hollywood Haunted: A Ghostly Tour of Filmland*. Los Angeles: Angel City Press, 1999.

Kouri, Michael. *The Most Haunted Places in Azusa*. Burbank, Calif.: Tapestry Autumn Press, 2001.

Lamb, John J. *San Diego Specters: Ghosts, Poltergeists, and Phantastic Tales*. El Cajon, Calif.: Sunbelt Publications, 1999.

MacKenzie, Andrew. *Hauntings and Apparitions*. London: Granada Publishing, 1982.

Marinacci, Mike. *Mysterious California: Strange Places and Eerie Phenomena in the Golden State*. Los Angeles, Calif.: Panpipes Press, 1988.

May, Alan. *The Legend of Kate Morgan: The Search for the Ghost of the Hotel del Coronado*. San Marcos, Calif.: Elk Publishing, 1990.

May, Antoinette. *Haunted Houses of California: A Ghostly Guide*. San Carlos, Calif.: World Wide Publishing, 1990.

Myers, Arthur. *The Ghostly Register: Haunted Dwellings—Active Spirits; A Journey to America's Strangest Landmarks*. Chicago: Contemporary Books, 1986.

Moody, Raymond A., Jr. *Life After Life*. Atlanta: Mockingbird Books, 1975.

Price, Harry. *Confessions of a Ghost Hunter*. New York: Causeway Books, 1974.

Ramsland, Katherine. *Ghost: Investigating the Other Side*. New York: St. Martin's Press, 2001.

Reinstedt, Randall. *Ghost Tales and Mysterious Happenings of Old Monterey.* Carmel, Calif.: Ghost Town Publications, 1977.

——. *Ghostly Tales of Old Monterey.* Carmel, Calif.: Ghost Town Publications, 1991.

Rogo, Scott. *Mind Beyond.* New York: Penguin Books, 1978.

——. *An Experience of Phantoms.* New York: Penguin Books, 1974.

——. *The Poltergeist Experience.* New York: Penguin Books, 1979.

Rule, Leslie. *Coast to Coast Ghosts: True Stories of Hauntings Across America.* Kansas City, Mo.: Andrews McMeel, 2001.

Senate, Richard. *Ghosts of the Haunted Coast.* San Diego: Pathfinder Publishing, 1986.

——. *Ghost Stalker's Guide to Haunted California.* Ventura, Calif.: Charon Press, 1998.

——. *The Haunted Southland: Ghosts of Southern California.* Ventura, Calif.: Charon Press, 1994.

Smith, Barbara. *Ghost Stories of California.* Auburn, Wash.: Lone Pine Publishing, 2001.

Southall, Richard. *How to Be a Ghost Hunter.* St. Paul, Minn.: Llewellyn Publications, 2003.

Taylor, Troy. *Ghost Hunter's Guidebook: The Essential Guide to Investigating Ghosts & Hauntings.* Alton, Ill.: Whitechapel Productions, 1999.

Tyrell, G. N. M. *Apparitions.* New York: Collier Books, 1963.

Underwood, Peter. *The Ghost Hunter's Guide.* Poole, England: Blandford Press, 1986.

Warren, Ed, and Lorraine Warren. *Ghost Hunters.* New York: St. Martin's Press, 1989.

Warren, Joshua P. *How to Hunt for Ghosts: A Practical Guide.* New York: Simon and Schuster Adult, 2003.

Wlodarski, Robert, Anne Wlodarski, and Michael Kouri. *Haunted Alcatraz.* Long Beach, Calif.: G-Host Publishing, 1998.

Wlodarski, Robert, and Anne Wlodarski. *Guide to the* Haunted Queen Mary. Long Beach, Calif.: G-Host Publishing 2000.

——. *Haunted Catalina.* Long Beach, Calif.: G-Host Publishing 1996.

Wood, Ted. *Ghosts of the West Coast: The Lost Souls of the* Queen Mary *and Other Real-life Hauntings.* New York: Walker and Co., 1999.

ARTICLES

"A-Haunting We Will Go to See All the Ghosts." *San Diego Union-Tribune.* 31 October 2002.

Associated Press. "Ghostbuster: Ohio Woman Inspires CBS' Supernatural Series." *Boston Herald,* 4 July 2005.

Associated Press. "L.A.'s Open-Scare Theatre: Film Fans Enjoy the Dearly Departed at Hollywood Forever Cemetery. *Daily Republic,* 23 August 2004.

Austin, Paige. "Psychic Society Will Seek Out Spirits in Old Towne." *Orange County Register,* 3 March 2001.

———. "Psychics Investigate Old Towne." *Orange County Register,* 8 March 2001.

Barrett, Greg. "Can the Living Talk to the Dead? Psychics Say They Connect with the Other World, but Skeptics Respond: "Prove it." *USA Today,* 20 June 2001.

"Borden House Exudes Allure of Macabre." *San Jose Mercury News,* 15 October 1995.

Burelison, S. "No Cheat Sheets in Ghostly Quiz." *San Diego Union-Tribune,* 31 October 2000.

Cadden, Mary. "Get Spooked on a Walking Tour." *USA Today,* 17 October 2003.

Carney, J. W. "Ghost Writer." *Pasadena Star-News,* 30 October 2002.

Carson, C. "A Boat's Capone Connection May Not Hold Water." *Ventura County Star,* 19 July 2004.

Clifford, Jane. "Shiver Me Timbers." *San Diego Union-Tribune,* 19 October 2002.

Davila, S. "Ghostly Gatherings." *Pasadena Star-News,* 30 October 2002.

———. "House Ghost Shown the Door." *Pasadena Star-News,* 31 October 2002.

Dean, Paul. "Voyage of the Ghost Ship *Queen Mary.*" *Los Angeles Times,* 11 June 1988.

Deffner, Elisabeth. "Reporter's Notebook: Shedding Light on Mysterious Goings-on at the Victorian Manor." *Orange County Register,* 25 October 2001.

Farren, Julie. "Bed, Breakfast, and Secrets." *San Bernardino Sun,* 19 August 1999, Living Section.

Ferrell, David. "Surroundings: *Queen Mary:* 'Gray Ghost' Harbors Some Tales." *Los Angeles Times,* 14 February 2002.

Fox, Carol. "Ghostbuster to Tell Secrets of the Hunt." *Los Angeles Times,* 28 October 1989.

"Ghostly Vibes." *Santa Barbara News-Press,* 31 October 2004.

Gibson, William, and Chester King. "Native Americans: Skeletons in Playa Vista's Closet." *Los Angeles Times,* 20 June 2004.

Gornstein, Leslie. "A Jinx in a Box? Maybe Mischievous Spirits Do Haunt This Jewel Cabinet." *Los Angeles Times,* 25 July 2004.

Grose, Thomas. "Ghosts Scare Up Good Business in Britain." *USA Today,* 22 August 1996.

Hernandez, Daniel. "Little Shop of Santeria." *Los Angeles Times,* 7 July 2005.

Hill, Angela. "Paranormal Expert Says It's Not All Funny." *Oakland Tribune,* 18 October 2002.

Hulse, Jane. "Yacht with a Past Hosts Mystery Shows and Ghost." *Los Angeles Times,* 19 June 1997, Ventura County edition.

Hutchinson, L. "Pasadena, a Place of Lively Spirits." *Pasadena Star-News,* 29 October 2001.

LaFee, Scott. "Haunting Pro Goes on Ghostly Iron Ship." *San Diego Union-Tribune,* 31 October 2001.

——. "Ghost Busted: Home Study Course in Spirit Hunting Is Certifiable." *San Diego Union-Tribune,* 31 October 2002.

Loar, Russell. "She's There When Things Go Bump in the Night." *Los Angeles Times,* 26 May 1997.

Martin, Hugo. "Graveyard Shift Puts History Before Horror." *Los Angeles Times,* 29 October 2004.

Massingill, T. "Business of Ghost Busting." *Contra Costa Times,* 8 October 2000, section D5.

McManis, Sam. "The X-Files of Contra Costa: Paranormal Investigator Lloyd Auerback Shares Tales from the Dark Side." *San Francisco Chronicle,* 30 October 1998.

Moran, Gwen. "Real-Life Ghost Busters." *USA Today,* 31 October 2004, weekend edition.

Paterno, Susan. "Tours of a Haunted Ship." *Los Angeles Times,* 2 October 1997.

Pilcher, Steve. "Wine and Spirits." *San Francisco Chronicle,* 28 October 2004.

"Point of Fear, Beauty, Mystery." *Santa Barbara News-Press,* 19 July 2004.

Quintanilla, Michael. "Haunting for Haunting; Ghosts: The Specters of Dead Children and Even Mafiosos Are Said to Lurk About in L.A." *Los Angeles Times,* 30 October 1998.

Rasmussen, Cecila. "L.A. Then and Now: Only History and Ghosts at Hall of Justice." *Los Angeles Times,* 26 May 2002, home edition.

Ritto, Mike. "Ghost Story: Does Murder Victim Walk the Halls of Villa del Sol?" *Fullerton News-Tribune,* 26 October 2000.

Rogers, Rick. "*Star of India* Sails to a Birthday." *San Diego Union-Tribune,* 9 November 2003.

Schenden, Laurie. "Attractions: Scaring Up Some Business." *Los Angeles Times,* 15 June 2000.

Sens, Josh. "The Truth Is Out There—Somewhere." *Via* (May/June 2002).

"Spirits, Specters and Strange Sightings Abound at America's Most Haunted Hotels." *Los Angeles Times,* 15 October 2003.

Tonnegossa, Richard. "Haunt Jaunt: Do You Dare Tour Local Places Where the Scary Things Are?" *San Diego Union-Tribune,"* 25 October 2001.

Toth, Marina Lynn. "Local Haunts." *San Bernardino Sun,* 31 October 1994, Living section.

Wilkens, John. "She Sees Dead People: Author Uses Her Healing Spirit to Help Release Stuck Souls." *San Diego Union-Tribune,* 31 October 2000.

Films, DVDs, and Videos

Fictional films may provide you with information that will assist you in preparing yourself for a ghost hunt. This assistance ranges from putting you in the proper mood for ghost hunting to useful techniques for exploring haunted places and information about the nature of ghostly activity.

The Amityville Horror (1979). Directed by Stuart Rosenberg. Starring James Brolin and Margot Kidder.

The Canterville Ghost (1996, made for TV). Directed by Sidney MaCartney. Starring Patrick Stewart.

Carrie (1976). Directed by Brian De Palma. Starring Sissy Spacek and Piper Laurie.

Cemetery Man (1994). Directed by Michele Soavi. Starring Rupert Everett and Francois Hadji-Lazaro.

Changeling (1980). Directed by Peter Medak. Starring George C. Scott and Trish VanDevere.

City of Angels (1998). Directed by Brad Silberling. Starring Nicolas Cage and Meg Ryan.

Dragonfly (2002). Directed by Tom Shadyac. Starring Kevin Costner and Kathy Bates.

The Entity (1983). Directed by Sidney J. Furie. Starring Barbara Hershey and Ron Silver.

Frighteners (1996). Directed by Peter Jackson. Starring Michael J. Fox and Trini Alvarado.

Ghosts of California. Documentary (2003).

Ghost of Flight 409 (1987, made for TV). Directed by Steven Hilliard Stern. Starring Ernest Borgnine and Kim Bassinger.

Ghost (1990). Directed by Jerry Zucker. Starring Patrick Swayze and Demi Moore.

Ghosts of England and Belgrave Hall (2001). The ISPR. Documentary.

Ghost Story (1981). Directed by John Irvin. Starring Fred Astaire and Melvyn Douglas.

Ghost Stories, Vol. 1 (1997). Documentary hosted by Patrick McNee.

Haunted (1995). Directed by Lewis Gilbert. Starring Aidan Quinn and Kate Beckinsale.

Haunted History. History Channel Home Video, 2-video set, 100 minutes.

Haunted Houses. A & E Home Video, 100 minutes.

Haunting (1999). Directed by Jan De Bont. Starring Liam Neeson and Catherine Zeta-Jones.

Haunting Across America. Documentary (2001). Produced by Linda Lewis. Hosted by Michael Dorn.

Haunting of Hell House (1999). Directed by Mitch Marcus. Starring Michael York and Claudia Christian.

Haunted History of Halloween. History Channel Home Video, 50 minutes.

Haunted Places. Documentary (2001). Filmmaker Christopher Lewis.

Haunting of Julia (1976). Directed by Richard Loncraine. Starring Mia Farrow and Keir Dullea.

Haunting of Morella (1991). Directed by Jim Wynorski. Starring David McCallum and Nicole Eggert.

Haunting of Sarah Hardy (1989). Directed by Jerry London. Starring Sela Ward, Michael Woods, and Morgan Fairchild.

Haunting of Seacliff Inn (1995). Directed by Walter Klenhard. Starring Ally Sheedy and William R. Moses.

Heartland Ghost (2002). Directed by Brian Trenchard-Smith. Starring Randy Birch and Beau Bridges.

Hollywood Ghosts and Gravesites. Documentary (2003).

Lady in White (1988). Directed by Frank LaLoggia. Starring Lukas Haas and Len Cariou.

Legend of Hell House (1998). Directed by John Hough. Starring

Pamela Franklin, Roddy MacDowell, and Clive Revill.

The Others (2001). Directed by Alejandro Amenabar. Starring Nicole Kidman and Christopher Eccleston.

Poltergeist (1982). Directed by Tobe Hooper. Starring JoBeth Williams and Craig T. Nelson.

Poltergeist II: The Other Side (1986). Directed by Brian Gibson. Starring JoBeth Williams and Craig T. Nelson.

Restless Spirits (1999). Directed by David Wellington. Starring Lothaire Bluteau, Michel Monty, and Marsha Mason.

Sightings: Ghost Reports (1998). By the producers of the TV show *Sightings*.

The Sixth Sense (1999). Directed by M. Night Shyamalan. Starring Bruce Willis and Haley Joel Osment.

The Unexplained: Hauntings. A & E Home Video, 50 minutes.

White Noise (2005). Directed by Geoffrey Sax. Starring Michael Keaton.

Internet Sources

www.theshadowlands.net/ghost

www.london-ghost-walk.co.uk

www.hauntings.com

www.historichotels.nationaltrust.org

www.paranormal.com

www.ghost-stalker.com (Web site for ghost hunter Richard Senate)

www.ghostweb.com/

www.ghosttowns.com

www.ghostbusters.com

www.the-atlantic-paranormal-society.com

www.hollowhill.com

www.Yahoo.com (For maps and driving instructions to a site, click on "MAPS." Enter your address [or any starting point], then enter the address of the haunted place you wish to visit. Yahoo will generate a free map and driving instructions, including an estimate of driving time and total miles.)

www.psiapplications.com/

www.TAPS.com (The Atlantic Paranormal Society)

www.historychannel.com

www.winchestermysteryhouse.com (Winchester Mystery House of San Jose)

www.ghostresearch.com

www.laparanormal.com

www.californiahistory.org (Links with State Historic Parks)

www.prarieghosts.com/ghostbooks.htlml

www.NPS.gov (National Park Service; locations include many historic sites)

www.meetup.com (Connects you with other paranormal investigators who meet monthly at L.A. locations to discuss common interests.)

www.technica.com (This is a catalog of electronic detectors and recorders used in ghost hunting.)

www.mindreader.com

www.OCPRgroup.com (Orange County Paranormal Research Group)

www.sdparanormal.com (San Diego Paranormal Research Project)

www.SGVPR.org (San Gabriel Valley Paranormal Researchers)

Organizations

American Society for Psychical Research
5 West Seventy-third Street
New York, NY 10023
(212) 799-5050

Bay Area Skeptics
P.O. Box 60
Concord, CA 94522

Berkeley Psychic Institute
2436 Hastings Street
Berkeley, CA 94704
(510) 548-8020

British Society for Psychical Research
Eleanor O'Keffe, secretary
49 Marloes Road
London W8 6LA
44-020-7937-8984

Center for Applied Intuition
2046 Clement Street
San Francisco, CA 94121

Center for Scientific Anomalies Research
P.O. Box 1052
Ann Arbor, Michigan 48103

Central Premonitions Registry
P.O. Box 482
Times Square Station
New York, NY 10036

Committee for Scientific Investigations of Claims of the Paranormal
1203 Kensington Avenue
Buffalo, NY 14215

Department of Psychology
Jordan Hall, Building 420
Stanford University
Stanford, CA 94305

Division of Parapsychology
Box 152, Medical Center
Charlottesville, VA 22908

Ghosttowns
www.ghosttowns.com

Graduate Parapsychology Program
John F. Kennedy University
12 Altarinda Road
Orinda, CA 94563
(415) 254-0200

Institute for Noetic Sciences
2658 Bridgewood
Sausalito, CA 94965

Institute for Parapsychology
Box 6847
College Station
Durham, NC 27708

International Ghost Hunter's Organization
www.ghostweb.com/ondex.html

International Society for Paranormal Research
4712 Admiralty Way
Marina del Rey, CA 90292

Office of Paranormal Investigations
JFK University
12 Altarinda Road
Orinda, CA 94563
(415) 249-9275

Orange County Paranormal Research Group
www.ocprgroup.com
E-mail: OCPR@OCPRgroup.com

Parapsychology Foundation
228 East Seventy-first Street
New York, NY 10021
(212) 628-1550

Parapsychology Research Group
3101 Washington Street
San Francisco, CA 94115

PSI Applications/Steve Moreno
Fairfield, CA
www.psiapplications.com
(707) 425-4382

Psychical Research Foundation
C/o William Roll
Psychology Department
West Georgia College
Carrolton, GA 30118

San Diego Paranormal Research Project
www.SDparanormal.com
E-mail: Info@SDparanormal.com

San Gabriel Valley Paranormal Researchers
511 South First Avenue # 175
Arcadia, CA 91006-6104
www.SGVPR.org

Saybrook Institute
1772 Vallejo Street
San Francisco, CA 94111-1920

Spiritual Emergency Network
California Institute of Transpersonal Psychology
250 Oak Grove Avenue
Menlo Park, CA 94025
(510) 327-2776

Society for Psychical Research
1 Adam and Eve Mewes
Kensington W8 6UG
England

Southern California Society for Psychical Research
269 South Arden Boulevard
Los Angeles, CA 90004

Special Tours and Events

Fullerton Haunted Walking Tour. Visit the local police station, Villa del Sol, the Plummer Auditorium, and many more haunted sites. Tour starts at 6:00 P.M. Wednesdays and Thursdays. Fee: $12.00.

Contact: Fullerton Museum Center
(714) 738-6545
www.fullertonmuseum.com

Haunted Hollywood Tours. Starts at Grauman's Chinese Theatre on Hollywood Boulevard. This tour takes you to the most fascinating places in Hollywood with a knowledgeable and entertaining guide.

Contact: Haunted Hollywood
6675 Hollywood Boulevard
Los Angeles, CA 90028-6220
(818) 415-8269
www.hauntedhollywoodtours.com

Ghost and Gravestones Tour. This is a trolley tour of several haunted places, including the famous Whaley House. Starts at 6:30 P.M. year-round.

Contact: San Diego Trolley Tours
849 West Harbor Drive
San Diego, CA 92101
(619) 298-8687

Haunted Hollywood Ghost Walk. Guided tours of several haunted sites with special emphasis on Hollywood's unique history from the 1930s to the 1950s.

Contact: Hollywood Ghost Walk
5752 Virginia Avenue Suite 109
Los Angeles, CA 90038
(323) 460-4787

***Queen Mary's* Shipwreck Halloween Terror Fest.** For 13 nights in October, the magnificent *Queen Mary* is transformed into a ghost ship complete with blood-splattered walls, grisly corpses, and spooky passageways. Bands, food, and drink make this a wild way to celebrate Halloween.

Contact: *Queen Mary*
13 Nights of Halloween
Long Beach, CA 9435-3511
www.queenmary.com

Queen Mary Tours hosts three great tours that focus on paranormal events.

Ghost Encounters Tour with Peter James. Tour the *Queen* with one of the most respected and experienced ghost hunters, Peter James. This one-hour tour takes you to several paranormal hot spots including the first-class pool, engine room, and Royal Theatre.

Contact: www.queenmary.com

Ghosts and Legends of the *Queen Mary.* This is a special-effects, walk-through show that dramatizes documented paranormal events and phenomena and historic events that have led to hauntings. This tour is a great way to become familiar with the ship's history and focus your ghost hunts to particular sites, people, or events.

Contact: www.queenmary.com

Haunted Encounters: The *Queen Mary's* Mysteries Revealed. This tour starts with an introductory lecture and short film, then continues with a one-hour walking tour.

Contact: www.queenmary.com

***Star of India* Tours.** Special tours are conducted in the evenings during the week of Halloween. The grand old ship is decked out with shredded sails and other props to make this a "ghost ship."

Contact: Maritime Museum of San Diego
1492 North Harbor Drive
San Diego, CA 92101
(619) 234-9153
www.sdmaritime.com

Hollywood Forever Cemetery Classic Movies. Enjoy classic films projected on the wall of a huge mausoleum while you relax under the celestial stars and over dead movie stars. Yes, you can lounge among the graves of Cecil B. DeMille, Douglas Fairbanks, Jr., Rudolph Valentino, and 88,000 others, sip wine, munch fancy foods, and savor Hollywood's golden era in film. Summer weekends.

Contact: Hollywood Forever Cemetery
6000 Santa Monica Boulevard
Los Angeles, CA 90038
(323) 469-1181
www.hollywoodforever.com
webmaster@forevernetwork.com.

Dia De Los Muertos (Day of the Dead). Olvera Street and El Pueblo Historical Monument, Los Angeles. Two weeks of events and celebrations from late October through early November. Highlights include screening of a video entitled "Day of the Dead" and history presentations that offer clues for ghost hunters. Several historic buildings comprising the El Pueblo Historical Monument are open and staffed by docents and history buffs.

Contact: Olvera Street Merchants
Los Angeles, CA 90001
(213) 625-0184 or (213) 625-7074

Marylyn Monroe Grave-side Memorial. Each year on August 5 a memorial is held at the gravesite of this famous movie star. Reservations are not necessary; no fee is required. Participants should respect the nature of this event and the rights of other attendees.

Contact: Westwood Village Memorial Park Cemetery
1218 Glendon Avenue
Los Angeles, CA 90024
(310) 474-1579

Pink Lady Watch. This is an informal gathering of ghost hunters and other curious folks who hope to see an apparition known as the Pink Lady. She appears on June 15 of every even-numbered year.

Contact: There is no organization coordinating this event.
Call 714-528-4260 for general information about the cemetery, located at 6749 Parkwood Court (major cross streets are Esperanza Road and Fairlynn Boulevard), Yorba Linda 92886. Also contact: Yorba Linda Chamber of Commerce at (714) 993-9537.

Richard Senate's Ghosts and Ghouls Tour. Led by one of the country's most respected ghost hunters, these tours focus on Ventura County.

Contact: Richard Senate
(805) 641-3844
www.ghost-stalker.com

Historical Societies and Museums

Historical societies and museums are good places to discover information about old houses and other buildings or places that figure prominently in local history. They often contain records in the form of old newspapers and diaries about tragic events such as fires, hangings, train wrecks, and earthquakes that led to the loss of life. Old photographs and maps may be available to serious researchers that are not on display for public viewing.

Arcadia Historical Society
380 West Huntington Drive
Arcadia, CA 991007
(626) 446-8512

Beverly Hills Historical Society
P.O. Box 1919
Beverly Hills, CA 90213
(818) 841-6333

Burbank Historical Society
1015 West Olive Avenue
Burbank, CA 91506
(808) 841-6333

Calabasas Historical Society
P.O. Box 8067
Calabasas, CA 91371
(818) 347-0470

Catalina Island Museum
1 Casino Way
Avalon, CA 90704
(310) 510-2414

Chatsworth Historical Society
10385 Shadow Oak Drive
Chatsworth, CA 91311
(818) 882-5614

Dana Point Historical Society
34085 Pacific Coast Highway
   #104
Dana Point, CA 92629
(949) 248-8121

El Pueblo de Los Angeles
  Historic Park
845 North Alameda Street
Los Angeles, CA 90012
(213) 628-3562

Fort MacArthur Museum
34601 South Gaffey Street
San Pedro, CA 90731
(310) 241-0846

Glendale Historical Society
P.O. Box 4173
Glendale, CA 912122
(818) 242-7447

Historical Society of Long
  Beach
210 East Ocean Boulevard
Long Beach, CA 90802
(562) 495-1210

Historical Society of Pomona
491 East Arrow Highway
Pomona, CA 91767
(909) 620-0264

Historical Society of Southern
  California
200 East Avenue 43
Los Angeles, CA 90031
(323) 222-0546

Hollywood History Museum
166 North Highland Avenue
Los Angeles, CA 90028
(213) 464-7776

La Jolla Historical Society
7846 Eads Avenue
La Jolla, CA 92037
(858) 459-5335

Monrovia Historical Society
215 East Lime Avenue
Monrovia, CA 91016-2832
(626) 358-0803

Muller House Museum
1542 South Beacon Street
San Pedro, CA 90731
(310) 831-1788

Redondo Beach Historical
  Society
P.O. Box 978
Redondo Beach, CA 90277
(310) 372-0197

Rialto Historical Society
205 North Riverside Blvd.
Rialto, CA 92376
(909) 875-1750

San Diego Historical Society
1649 El Prado # 3
San Diego, CA 92101
(619) 232-6203

Santa Ana Historical Society
120 Civic Center Drive West
Santa Ana, CA 92701
(714) 547-9645

Santa Barbara History Museum
2559 Puesta del Sol
Santa Barbara, CA 93105
(805) 682-3224

Santa Inez Historical Society
3596 Sagunto Street
Santa Inez, CA 93460
(805) 688-7889

Santa Maria Historical Society
616 South Broadway
Santa Maria, CA 93454
(805) 922-3130

Torrance Historical Society
1345 Post Avenue
Torrance, CA 90501
(310) 328-5392

Venice Historical Society
P.O. Box 12844
Marina del Rey, CA 90295
(313) 967-5170

Venture County Museum of
   History
100 East Main Street
Ventura, CA 93001
(805) 653-0323

Wells Fargo History Museum
333 South Grand Avenue
Los Angeles, CA 90071
(213) 253-7166

Wilmington Historical Society
309 West Opp Street
P.O. Box 1435
Wilmington, CA 90748
(313) 835-8239

Index

Praise for the first book in Jeff Dwyer's
Ghost Hunter's Guide Series

Ghost Hunter's Guide to the San Francisco Bay Area

"I am thoroughly impressed with Jeff Dwyer's *Ghost Hunter's Guide* and would recommend it to all, from total novice to professional investigator."   —Steven Moreno, president, PSI Applications

"This is a book that is a good guide to its subject, but it is also a pleasant read, even if you seldom leave your chair!"
                            —Dan Hays, *Portland (OR) Statesman Journal*

"Fans of hauntings and ghost stories who are heading towards San Francisco (and the surrounding areas) will love this comprehensive guide to the Bay Area's most eerie spots."   —Fabuloustravel.com

"Ghost stories in the area chronicled in Dwyer's book . . . while sometimes scary, more often serve as reminders of the sometimes quirky, and oftentimes tragically haunting, history of the people of California."   —TheReporter.com (Vacaville, CA)

"A handy ghost hunter's 'how-to' guide . . . I thought I knew everything about the wine country, but I apparently overlooked the protoplasmic 'walk by night' world."
                            —Mick Winter, author of *The Napa Valley Book*

"Unveils the spooky side of the City by the Bay."
                            —*The Sun* magazine

Ghost Hunter's Guide to the San Francisco Bay Area

Ghost Hunter's Guide to the San Francisco Bay Area highlights more than one hundred haunted spots in and around San Francisco, all accessible to the public, where you can research and organize your own ghost hunt. Complete with handy checklists, procedural tips, and anecdotal evidence of previous sightings at each location, the guide is an inquisitive and informative supplement to—or replacement for—traditional tourist guidebooks of the Bay Area.

Whether readers visit familiar haunts such as Alcatraz, Angel Island, Fisherman's Wharf, or lesser-known locations such as the USS *Hornet,* the Old Bodega Schoolhouse, or the First and Last Chance Saloon, all are sure to encounter places and consider possibilities unexplored by the average visitor. With advice on what to do with a ghost, what to do after the ghost hunt, and other telekinetic tidbits, this guide encourages travelers to be attentive and imaginative, willing to take that extra spirit-sighting step. For the curious armchair traveler, it is a lively twist on Bay Area history and landmarks.

176 pp. 5½ x 8½
28 photos Appendixes Index
9781589802896

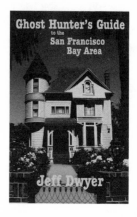

Ghost Hunter's Guide to New Orleans

Designed as a guide for locals, new residents, and travelers seeking encounters with the unique, off-the-beaten-path history of the Crescent City, this book will enable novice and experienced paranormal adventurers to see beyond the surface of the usual tourist haunts and historic sites. Detailed descriptions and historical background for more than two hundred locations guide readers to sites of various tragedies, criminal activities, and ghostly legends and lore throughout New Orleans and along the lower Mississippi River.

Suggested stops include famous cemeteries such as St. Louis Cemetery #1 and Lafayette Cemetery # 1 and the former homes of Civil War notables like Confederate president Jefferson Davis and Gen. P.G.T. Beauregard. After visiting the spirits at world-famous bars and restaurants such as Commander's Palace and Arnaud's Restaurant, visitors may want to take a seat next to a ghost at the haunted Le Petit Théâtre du Vieux Carre. A short drive upriver, adventurous souls will find the world-famous Myrtles Plantation, reputed to be the most haunted house in America, and other beautiful remnants of the antebellum South, including the magnificent Oak Alley, San Francisco Plantation, and the Old State Capitol in Baton Rouge.

304 pp. 5½ x 8½
50 photos Appendixes Index
9781589804081

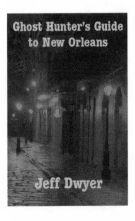

RELATED PELICAN TITLES

A Ghost Watcher's Guide to Ireland by John Dunne
Illustrated with the hauntingly beautiful photographs of world-renowned photographer Simon Marsden.
128 pp. 8 x 8 70 photos
9781565548985

Scottish Ghosts by Lily Seafield
Fairies, white ladies, tortured souls, poltergeists, malevolent phantoms, hideous creatures—Scotland has them all.
192 pp. 5¼ x 8 Index
9781565548435

The Haunting of Louisiana by Barbara Sillery
Photography by Oak Lea and Danielle Genter
Based on the PBS documentary, this book showcases many of the stories that would not fit into the one-hour television program.
224 pp. 5½ x 8½ 22 photos Biblio. Index
9781565549050

Alice Flagg: The Ghost of the Hermitage by Nancy Rhyne
The people of Murrell's Inlet, South Carolina, are haunted by the ghost of a 15-year-old planter's daughter—a legend that continues today.
256 pp. 6 x 9
9781589802698

Halloween: An American Holiday, an American History
0by Lesley Pratt Bannatyne
"By far the best book on the history of Halloween available today."
—Alison Guss, senior producer,
"The Haunted History of Halloween," The History Channel
192 pp. 6 x 9 4 illus. 24 photos Biblio. Index
9781565543461

Visit www.pelicanpub.com for more information on
these and other history, travel, and holiday titles.